Perspectives on Counseling Adults: Issues and Skills

Perspectives on Counseling Adults: Issues and Skills

Nancy K. Schlossberg
University of Maryland

Lillian E. Troll
Rutgers University

Zandy Leibowitz
University of Maryland

Brooks/Cole Publishing Company
Monterey, California
A Division of Wadsworth Publishing Company, Inc.

Acquisition Editor: Charles T. Hendrix
Manuscript Editor: Margaret C. Tropp
Production Editor: Micky Lawler
Interior Design: Jamie S. Brooks
Cover Design: Katherine Minerva
Typesetting: Daybreak Typesetting Services, Albany, N.Y.

Printed in the United States of America

10 9 8 7 6 5 4 3 2 1

Library of Congress Cataloging in Publication Data

Schlossberg, Nancy K
    Perspectives on counseling adults.

    Bibliography: p. 143
    Includes index.
    1. Adulthood. 2. Counseling. I. Troll, Lillian
E., joint author. II. Leibowitz, Zandy,
joint author. III. Title.
BF724.5.S35   158   77-16292
ISBN 0-8185-0261-4

Preface

The adult years, once thought to be a time of stability and rationality, are now recognized as a period of change and uncertainty. Both the minor problems of daily life and the major transitions experienced by virtually all human beings can result in times of crisis and stress for people in the 20-to-60 age range. Often, however, people are unprepared for such transitions because they have been taught that "adultness" represents a state of sameness and saneness. Thus, they may feel isolated and confused by their own feelings, not recognizing that these feelings are virtually universal. These adults are not seriously disturbed individuals who require psychotherapy. The problems they face are normal, but they sometimes need help in dealing with them. Providing that help is the function of the counselor of adults.

It is our belief that counselors of adults need both a thorough knowledge of the major issues of adult development and special skills not required by general educational/vocational guidance counselors, who usually deal with children and adolescents. This book is directed, then, at students in training as counselors, teachers, social workers, and community aides—as well as at practitioners—in the hope of helping them develop their knowledge and skills. It can be used in conjunction with *Counseling Adults,* a book of readings edited by Nancy K. Schlossberg and Alan D. Entine (Brooks/Cole, 1977).

The book is divided into two major parts—Issues and Skills—with five chapters in each. Each chapter in the first part provides information on the issues and corresponds to a chapter in the second part that reviews the earlier material and offers activities designed to give training in skills. Thus, Chapter 1, "Recognition and Control of Age Bias," discusses the issue of age bias, the forms it takes, its causes, its dangers, and the ways in which it may be overcome. Chapter 6, "Recognizing and Combating Age Bias," offers a number of activities whereby the information in the earlier chapter can be put to work. Some of the activities are designed to be performed by the individual working alone, and others are designed to be performed in a group setting. The activities and skills presented in Part Two provide examples that can be used by instructors to create additional or alternative learning formats of their own.

Part Two, on skills, was developed by the

National Consortium on Competency-Based Staff Development, in Cooperation with the American Institutes for Research, under support by the United States Office of Education, Department of Health, Education and Welfare, under Part C of the Vocational Education Act of 1963. We appreciate the cooperation and help of members of the guidance staff at Prince George's Community College and Montgomery Community College. These colleagues spent several days with us in a pilot- and field-test of the activities in the Skills section.

We would also like to acknowledge the assistance of our reviewers, who offered many helpful suggestions: Helen V. Collier of Indiana University, John Dahl of California State University at Los Angeles, Joan England of the University of South Dakota, Alan D. Entine of the State University of New York at Stony Brook, Janet Heddesheimer of The George Washington University, Mark Meadows of Auburn University, Daniel Sinick of The George Washington University, David Tiedeman of Northern Illinois University, and Thelma Jones Vriend of Wayne County Community College.

A major part of the integration of this book was done by Laura Kent. We cannot thank her enough for her superior editing. Without her ready comprehension of the essential statement we were trying to make, as well as her firmness in insisting on procedures that would highlight and clarify this statement, we would probably still be stumbling.

Nancy K. Schlossberg
Lillian E. Troll
Zandy Leibowitz

Contents

PART ONE

Issues

1

Recognition and Control of Age Bias

If counselors can be said to have a creed, it is that we regard all clients as individuals, that we look for their unique qualities, that we do not prejudge them. Whatever the stereotypes common in our society—whether of sex, color, ethnic background, or social class—we as counselors are supposed to be free of them. Yet how can we reach this point of particularized attention to the individual client when all our lives, from about age 2, we have categorized everyone we meet according to sets of obvious characteristics and have made assumptions, derived from our past experiences with other people having these characteristics, about the attitudes, values, and other traits of new acquaintances?

To some extent, these assumptions are useful, serving as preliminary steps in getting to know people. Indeed, as Goffman (1963) has pointed out, we could not survive if we had to approach every situation *de nova*. Categorizations and classifications enable us to process situations quickly and to react efficiently, as if by instinct. The danger arises when we categorize on the basis of irrelevant factors, when we fail to recognize that we are categorizing,

or when we make unwarranted value judgments on the basis of our categorization. The counselor must be constantly aware of the tendency to categorize and continuously willing to revise initial assumptions as more information is acquired.

In the last decade or so, most Americans have become sensitive to the tendency to prejudge people on the basis of their racial/ethnic background. Whole sets of once-automatic and unquestioned assumptions—about Blacks, about Chicanos, about Polish-Americans, about Italian-Americans—have been exposed as oversimplifications at best, generalizations that do not fit particular cases. Although it cannot be said that everyone in this country is now free of such prejudice, most people are at least aware that it is open to challenge. More recently, people have begun to look at their deep-seated stereotypes based on sex. Again, although most people have not rid themselves entirely of sex bias or been willing to jettison the traditional view of sex roles, they now realize that such beliefs are not universally accepted. There is one area of bias, however, that people continue to overlook, and that is stereotyping based on age.

3

Almost all societies have rules and customs based on age (and sex as well) that decree what males and females at different ages should do or not do and how they should behave toward one another. In some parts of the world, age grading is a fundamental part of the social structure; people may even take different names and live in different places at different times of their lives, in accordance with their age status. In such societies, the rules are explicit and rigid. Superficially, our society is much more flexible in specifying what people should be like and how they should behave at any particular age. But this flexibility is only relative. Bernice L. Neugarten has done extensive research on the age norms and age constraints that operate in our society. One study (Neugarten, Moore, & Lowe, 1965) found remarkable agreement among respondents of different ages about what age is appropriate for a particular behavior. For example, at least four in five of the respondents believed that the best age for a man to marry is between 20 and 25, for a woman between 19 and 24; that people should finish school and go to work between 20 and 22; that people should retire between 60 and 65. These convictions about age-appropriate behavior may be just as strong as, or even stronger than, convictions about sex-appropriate behavior.

Neugarten (1977) postulates that "there exists a socially prescribed timetable for the ordering of major life events" (p. 34)* and that most adults conform to this timetable. Although adulthood is not marked by the dramatic biological changes that trigger psychological development in childhood and adolescence, most adults have built-in "social clocks" by which they judge whether they are "on time" in particular life events. To be "off time," whether early or late, is to be age deviant; and, like any other kind of deviance, this carries with it social penalties. The woman not married by age 29 used to —and maybe still does—feel ashamed. The man who is still in school at age 30 feels ashamed. It is as shameful to have a baby at age 45 as at age 15. Furthermore, age norms differ for men and women. Women are expected (both by themselves and by others) to date, to marry, and to have children at an earlier age than men. Neugarten concludes that, in considering social expectations about appropriate behavior, one should think in terms of age/sex roles, rather than just age roles or sex roles.

The term *agism* (Butler, 1969) has been used to refer to the stereotyping of old people, who in our society are generally regarded as inferior and useless human beings. But the term can be applied with equal force to the stereotyping of any age group. *Agism,* or *age bias,* may be defined as assumptions made about people purely on the basis of their age. It consists of a whole network of myths—unsubstantiated beliefs that may be a combination of fact and falsehood and that influence our interaction with others. The premise is that, because we know a person's age, we can with fair accuracy predict his/her abilities, values, interests, and behavior. Age bias can take three forms (Troll & Nowak, 1976):

restrictiveness: the belief that certain behaviors are appropriate at certain ages and inappropriate at others: for example, 25-year-olds should be embarked on their careers; 60-year-olds should not become doctoral candidates. Evidence indicates that attitudes toward younger adults tend to be more restrictive than attitudes toward older adults.

distortion: lack of congruence between the charac-

*From "Adaptation and the Life Cycle," by B. L. Neugarten. In N. K. Schlossberg and A. D. Entine (Eds.), *Counseling Adults.* © 1977 by Wadsworth Publishing Company, Inc. This and all other quotations from this source are reprinted by permission of the publisher, Brooks/Cole Publishing Company.

teristics that "outsiders" ascribe to an age group and the characteristics that the age group ascribes to itself. For example, it is widely assumed that middle-aged women are bereft when the last child leaves home (the "empty-nest" syndrome). Recent research shows, however, that most of these women experience a tremendous sense of relief and well-being at this time. Age distortion results from holding certain stereotyped attitudes toward age groups; in this case, the attitudes happen to be wrong.

negative attitudes: unfavorable or hostile attitudes toward any age group: for example, seeing all teenagers as rude and loud; seeing all older people as dependent or as bad-tempered.

Agism begins in early childhood. Three-year-olds say the word *old* means "yucky" or "throw it away; don't touch it!" (Treybig, 1974). When Ahammer and Baltes (1972) asked three age groups (high school students, adults, and old people) to describe themselves and the other two age groups, they found that misperception of the other age groups was common: the young adults and older adults said that teenagers were wilder and more radical than they actually were, whereas the teenagers said that older people were more conservative and rigid than they actually were.

Considerable research has been done on prevalent age stereotypes. The common myths about young adults are that they are autonomous and free to choose their own goals (Bortner & Hultsch, 1974), that they are exuberant and independent, high in drive to achieve and low in desire to be taken care of (Aaronson, 1966). Therefore, when 25-year-old men and women find themselves apathetic and fatigued, depressed by the limited circumstances of their lives, they are doubly depressed: first, by their life situation; and, second, by the guilty conviction that they are "off time" for not being autonomous and exuberant. They hate to ask the advice of others before making difficult deci-

sions because they are supposed to be independent. If they enjoy being quiet nonachievers, they suspect there is something wrong with them for not being strivers after success. They may want comfort from friends and family at times of sorrow and difficulty, but they will not let themselves ask for or accept it. All too often, they jump into roles for which they are not yet ready—deciding on a long-term career, getting married, having children—because not to do so is to brand themselves as age deviant, and that is unthinkable.

According to the myths, adults in the middle years are responsible, settled, and contented. They are at the peak of their accomplishment. They are starting to think about giving up roles rather than taking on new ones (except ancillary roles such as grandparent). It is too late for them to think of beginning new careers and of having or adopting children. But what of the adults in this age range who find that, instead of withdrawing, they feel more outgoing than ever; that instead of being content with their responsibilities, they have the urge to explore; that instead of settling down to accomplishment in their chosen career, they want to try a whole new career from the bottom up? These people are indeed in trouble, in their own eyes and in the eyes of the world.

At about age 60, people are supposed to become old men and old women, ready to retire from their jobs and to enter a kind of limbo. Old people are supposed to lose their health, their wits, and their income; to become dependent on their children (Neugarten & Garron, 1951); to be hopeless, helpless, and unattractive (Kahana, 1970). But what if they are in perfect health and smarter than they have ever been? What if they fall in love and want to divorce an old mate and marry a new one? What if they try to act on lifelong ambitions and want to work around the clock? What if they want to enjoy life freely and extravagantly, without depending on or accounting to others? Such people will find themselves in an uncomfortable bind, trapped not only by the expectations of others but by their own convictions about what constitutes right and proper behavior for old people.

The most insidious aspect of age stereotypes is that they are not imposed from above or from outside but, like all social stereotypes, are part of the belief system of the individual. People who find that they simply do not conform to the stereotype are inclined to feel not that the stereotype is wrong but that they themselves are somehow to blame. Fighting the stereotypes requires not only inner strength but also, frequently, outside help. And that is where the counselor comes into the picture.

Because counselors share the socialization of other Americans, it is almost inevitable that we also make assumptions about age-appropriate behavior. In short, we, too, are age biased. This fact—though difficult to face—is important in that the decisions confronting many of our clients are related directly to what is expected of them, by themselves and by others, because of their age (and their sex as well). Should they make do with an unsatisfactory way of life because at their age they can expect nothing better? Should they refrain from trying to make a fresh start—going back to school, taking up a new career, terminating an unhappy marriage—out of fear that they will make fools of themselves? It is for answers to questions such as these that adults turn to counselors for help.

As was pointed out earlier, experts on adult development believe that changes in adults are controlled more by social than by biological clocks. Even the severe upheavals of adolescence may be triggered not so much by the biological phenomenon known as puberty as by a shift in the expectations of others: they can no longer act like children; all of a sudden they must grow up. The implications of the social-clock metaphor are central to the functioning of counselors. Presumably, social conditions can be altered more easily than can biological conditions. What may have been appropriate at an earlier historical period, when medical, social, and economic conditions were different, is not necessarily appropriate today. Counselors must take a fresh look at the adult years. As we move away from the assumption that certain events are inevitable and right at certain ages, we can move toward helping our clients to explore new options at every age.

EXAMINING BIAS: THE AGE NORMS INQUIRY

The Age Norms Inquiry (ANI), a brief questionnaire derived from the previously mentioned study by Neugarten et al. (1965), was first introduced at a workshop for counselors of adults held by Nancy Schlossberg and Lillian Troll in the summer of 1968. It comprises three types of items: those relating to general characteristics, those relating to marriage and the family, and those relating to career. Half the items deal with men, and half with women. (A copy of the revised form appears in Chapter 6.)

Although the original intention was to use the ANI simply to illustrate a presentation on age stereotyping, it soon became clear that the workshop participants, who completed the form as an exercise, were by no means free of age bias. For instance, many believed that a man over 40—and a woman over 30—is no longer attractive; many felt that people should be finished with education and settled on a career by their mid-20s and that changing jobs in the middle years is "wrong." Had they been asked directly whether their counseling was influenced by a client's age, most would probably have said no. But confronted with the evidence of their own responses to the ANI, they had to admit to some degree of age bias.

Continued exploration with the ANI was carried out on various samples: college counselors, educators working with adults, students in counseling programs, and practitioners of other helping professions. However "sophisticated" or "enlightened" the group, about nine in ten of the members indicated age limits on some items. Occasionally a questionnaire would come back with a vigorous notation such as "Age has nothing to do with any of this!" scrawled across it, and a few respondents wrote angry letters protesting the whole notion of age stereotyping. But such reactions were rare.

Table 1-1 gives some indication of the degree of bias associated with selected items from an earlier form of the ANI. In general, the least age-stereotyped responses came from graduate students

TABLE 1-1. Proportion of respondents manifesting age bias in selected items from the Age Norms Inquiry

Item Type	Items	% Age Biased [a]	Women Less Age Biased [b]
Family	Men marry	83	X
Family	Women marry	83	
Career	Men decide on career	77	
Career	Men finish education	75	X
Career	Women finish education	71	
General	Women accomplish most	70	X
Family	Men live with parents	64	
Family	Women live with parents	64	
General	Middle-aged women	64	X
General	Middle-aged men	63	X
Career	Change from social worker to pilot	61	X
General	Young man	59	
General	Young woman	59	X
Career	Men retire	58	
General	Men accomplish most	58	X
Career	Men hold top job	55	X
Family	Women have another child	52	X
Career	Change from bus driver to sociologist	47	X
Career	Change from insurance to architecture	45	
Career	Change from teacher to lawyer	45	X
Career	Men run for public office	42	X
General	Attractive woman	42	X
General	Attractive man	37	X
General	Dance the "Funky Broadway"	32	
Career	Men change career	32	X
Career	Men return to college	26	X
Career	Women return to college	24	X
Career	Men move family for better job	23	X
Career	Change from executive to teacher	17	

[a]Respondent checked either of two younger age categories listed.
[b]χ^2 significant at .05 level or better.

in adult development and aging, particularly those who planned on careers as counselors of adults. But even in these groups, a majority held age stereotypes. The most age-biased respondents were people who worked with young children, particularly elementary school teachers but also child psychologists and psychiatrists, pediatric nurses, and children's social workers. A self-selection process may be operating: people who want to help their pupils or clients to change constructively but who feel that adulthood is a period of stasis will choose occupations that allow them to work with children; only those who feel that adults are open to change (and thus, who are also relatively free from age-stereotyped thinking) will choose careers that allow them to work with adults.

Different types of counselors of adults varied in age bias. Vocational rehabilitation counselors were among the most proscriptive. More than half of the college counselors in our national survey gave a substantial proportion of age-biased answers, and few of them gave none. What is even more disquieting, those counselors who had taken courses in counseling were no less age biased than those with no formal training; perhaps such courses inculcate "oughts" and "shoulds" so that trained counselors end up at least as biased as some of those who are untrained. A closely related study of students in counseling curricula (Schlossberg & Pietrofesa, 1973) found that sex bias was prevalent among prospective counselors, who often said they would advise their clients to follow sex-typed careers.

Some general conclusions can be drawn from studies with the ANI:

1. There is consensus among counselors of adults about age norms and age constraints. More than half manifested some age bias; indeed, they were free of bias on only one-third of the items. On the other hand, some counselors of adults who returned the questionnaire opposed any suggestion of age norms and argued that each case should be considered individually; it seems likely that many others who failed to complete and return the questionnaire were of like mind and that their nonresponse was a protest against a document that they regarded as endorsing age constraints. Thus, counselors who work with adults differ from the middle-class groups studied by Neugarten et al. (1965) in the direction of greater freedom from age proscriptions. If counselors are not entirely free of bias, neither are they as age biased as people in the general population.

2. Women counselors were generally less age biased than men counselors. Aside from sex, no observed characteristic—age, years of counseling experience, specialized training in counseling—was significantly related to age bias, though (as mentioned previously) specialized courses seemed to contribute to greater age bias.

3. Item type—general, family, career—was not related to degree of bias, but events at the inauguration of adulthood seemed to elicit more restrictiveness than events of later life. It seems harder for a person to go against age expectations in the 20s than in the 40s.

To summarize: although the results of these explorations with the Age Norms Inquiry were encouraging insofar as they indicated that counselors of adults are less age biased than the average American, they were far from reassuring in absolute terms.

IMPLICATIONS FOR COUNSELING

As was pointed out earlier, categories and stereotypes serve the function of enabling us to process new situations quickly and respond to them efficiently. They become dysfunctional under three conditions: (1) when they are based on irrelevant variables, (2) when they are applied unconsciously, and (3) when they have value labels attached to them. To expand on the last point: It seems to be a common tendency not only to categorize but also to rank-order different categories in terms of some value system. We are not content to differentiate A, B, and C; we must add that A is mediocre, B is slightly better, and C is the best. When we apply this process to human beings—when we say that one human being is not as good or as worthy as another because of his/her age or color or social class—the damage may be severe. Not only do we injure the individuals so categorized and so stigmatized, but we may also harm society by denying it the contributions that these people could make were they not damned a priori by such labeling.

Although the following statement (Bergmann, 1974) focuses on the illegality of sex discrimination in employment, it has a wider application:

> A great principle which has emerged from anti-discrimination legislation is that it is no longer permissible for an employer to treat any particular woman as if she were the "average woman." . . . The fact of life which the law recognizes is that all men are not, for purposes of work, different from all women; that there is a distribution of talents and propensities among men and women; and that these distributions, although not identical, do overlap [p. 2].

The point can be generalized as follows: it is not valid to treat any particular person as though that person were the "average" member of a group to which he/she belongs. The "average" Puerto Rican, the "average" physician, the "average" Methodist, the "average" homosexual, the "average" adolescent, the "average" philatelist—the average anything is a statistical fiction.

The implication for counselors of adults is obvious: the individual client can no longer be dealt with merely on the basis of chronological years. To

have generalized knowledge about the characteristics of a particular age group is one thing; to make assumptions drawn from that knowledge about the characteristics of an individual who happens to be in that age group is quite another. That approach can lead only to misperceptions, oversimplifications, and inequities.

It is our responsibility as counselors to present clients with options and to indicate the possible consequences of those options to the best of our knowledge. It is not part of our responsibility to tell clients that they should not take risks or that the choice of a particular option is wrong. For example, if women over 40 have a high probability of bearing abnormal children, then a 42-year-old female client who is thinking about becoming pregnant for the first time should be advised of this probability. To give information about the risks involved in late pregnancies so that women can plan their childbearing rationally is justified; indeed, it is part of the counselor's job. But to label a late pregnancy "wrong" is not justified. Human beings take risks every day of their lives, some knowingly, some blindly. To prevent competent people from making their own decisions goes against the fundamental principles of counseling.

The example just given, the timing of the first childbirth, is a common subject of age norms. Moreover, because it involves decisions about other aspects of life as well (such as the wife's employment outside the home, the couple's amount of leisure time), it is central to the planning of many young people. One often hears it said nowadays that a woman should have her first child in her 20s: either earlier or later is bad. But to what extent is this "rule" a physiological fact, and to what extent an age stereotype? Although women in their late 30s are more likely to bear defective children and to have difficulty carrying and delivering a child than are younger women, the leeway is considerably greater than one is led to believe by most advice texts. Nor in these days of amniocentesis and legal abortion is it necessary for a woman simply to play the odds when she becomes pregnant. Many women who are not ready to get married and many couples who are not ready for a child in their 20s or early 30s may be ready by their late 30s; the extra time allows for greater personal and career development before entry into the difficult early years of child rearing. Yet many couples go through a crisis of decision when the wife approaches age 29 that is, by and large, unnecessary.

Age norms and age constraints may cripple the individual in a variety of other ways as well. For instance, because one is supposed to finish one's education and start on a career by age 22, many young people make hurried decisions based on inadequate information about themselves and about the world of jobs and find themselves launched on careers that turn out to be unsuitable and unsatisfying. Once launched, however, they are reluctant even to consider changing occupations, especially since that may entail further schooling. To make such a change is to violate the prescriptive timetable, to fall behind schedule, to be off time.

Similarly, because age 65 is regarded as the appropriate time for retirement, many people stop working when they are at the height of their physical and mental powers. Having withdrawn from the very activities that gave their lives vigor and meaning, they find themselves consigned to an existence of meaningless boredom. Others who, at age 45, have achieved all their vocational goals and who yearn for a more leisurely lifestyle find themselves obliged to mark time for another 20 years.

The effective counselor, who realizes that age norms and age constraints operate to the detriment of many people, works to help clients free themselves of these constraints. As a first step, counselors —and others in the helping professions who work with adults—should take a close look at their own age bias. It is not easy for us, as social scientists and as (presumably) sophisticated and humane individuals, to admit the possibility of our own bias. If we do not, however, we as counselors will restrict rather than help free our clients.

Having admitted the possibility of one's own bias (whether age bias or any other kind), and having acknowledged that bias may result in unhappiness for large numbers of human beings, how does one go about overcoming or controlling that bias? At the outset, it must be recognized that categories are necessary not only for the organization of knowledge and the maintenance of social order but also for human functioning from moment to moment. Nonetheless, to categorize people may be to stigmatize them as well and thus to prevent them from reaching their full potential. Categorizations, as they are applied to people, must be constantly shaken up and questioned.

The question that counselors of adults should ask themselves in dealing with their clients is: am I willing to share the fate of those whom I currently exclude because of age? The thrust of counselor education should be to encourage self-examination on this question. The next chapter presents some empirical evidence showing that there need be no hard-and-fast rules as to what constitutes appropriate behavior at what chronological age. One's age need not impose strict limitations on one's options.

This last point can be illustrated by the story of a woman, a colleague of the authors, who was bright, attractive, motivated. Throughout her adult life, she had been active in the community, serving in such positions as president of the board of a mental health center and trustee of a community college, though she had never had professional training. Most of her leadership positions came to her because she was the wife of a successful man. When her husband died, she applied for admission to a doctoral program in counseling and guidance, eager to pursue a career in her own right. In view of her abilities and experience, it might seem that she would be instantly admitted into any such program. But at the time she applied, she was 62 years old. In most circumstances, a woman of this age would have almost no chance of being accepted, completing the doctoral program successfully, and becoming a practitioner. In this case, the admissions committee, after long and strenuous deliberation, admitted her to candidacy. She eventually received the doctorate, got a job in an adult counseling center, and was subsequently picked for a high-level position in the state government, initiating programs for older adults and the aged.

Her story is unusual because the woman herself is unusual; even more so is the decision of the admissions committee, whose members managed to see through the haze of age stereotypes to the individual woman. Such freedom from bias is still rare. Perhaps in the future people will come to recognize agism, as they now recognize racism and sexism, and decisions like this one will become more common.

For activities and skills related to this chapter, see Chapter 6.

2

Adulthood: Themes, Views, and Facts

Development in childhood is the subject not only of extensive empirical research but also of a solid body of theory. Until very recently, however, the middle and late years of life have been neglected by researchers and theorists. Part of the reason for this neglect is the assumption that adulthood is static, a period of stability and certainty during which no growth or development occurs. In the common view, people make their most important decisions before or during their mid-20s and then settle into a steady pattern of life, untroubled by the doubts, conflicts, and upheavals that mark their earlier years. This view may have made sense in an earlier historical period, when the average life span was much shorter, when society was more ordered and stable, and when the emphasis was on survival of the species and the social unit rather than on fulfillment of the individual. But the 20th century has rendered this view of adulthood untenable.

Consequently, we now see an upsurge of research interest in adulthood and aging. Biological and social scientists have been examining the dynamics of this later period of life in an attempt to discover what kinds of development take place and how they are triggered. Are there definable stages?

How closely related is change to chronological age? What personal and situational factors influence adult development? These are some of the questions currently being explored that have relevance to the work of counselors.

This chapter first discusses themes of adulthood, then describes the work of a number of major theorists and the assumptions that underlie that work, and finally presents some specific research information on development in the adult years.

THEMES OF ADULTHOOD

Adulthood is a period not of stability and certainty, as is often assumed, but of change and, in the view of the authors, of individual development, at least potentially. The changes that characterize infancy, childhood, and adolescence occur in relatively discrete and well-defined stages. In contrast, the changes that occur in adulthood have no absolute time or sequential order, though certain events are linked, by probability and by social expectation, to certain ages—for example, getting married in one's 20s, retiring in one's 60s. Different people may experience these changes at different times, or not at

13

all. Nonetheless, the pattern of adult life is characterized by periods of relative stability, bridged by transitions or turning points.

For instance, people typically graduate from high school, either take jobs or go on to college, and at some point terminate their education and take jobs; usually change jobs several times, either out of choice or because they are fired; sometimes return to school; get promoted or fail to be promoted; and eventually retire. All these shifts represent transitions or turning points in the arena of work (meaning both educational and occupational careers). In the area of interpersonal relations, young adults leave the parental home; get married and have children; make friends and lose them; sometimes get divorced or are widowed; see their children leave home.

Change may occur in other areas of life as well. For instance, in our geographically mobile society, most people make one or more residential changes during their lives, though the distances involved may vary from a move within the same neighborhood or city to a move across the world. Their leisure activities—from participation in civic or political groups to hobbies and sports—may alter. Over the course of the adult years, their physical condition may change drastically. Change in one area may precipitate, or be accompanied by, changes in others. Thus, the person who moves from one city to another usually changes jobs and also forms a new network of friendships. The woman who finds herself widowed may have to return to the labor force. The person who suffers a heart attack may be forced to retire early.

These events often involve new sets of relationships, new expectations, and altered self-evaluations. A distinction may be made between *role increments* (such as getting married, having a child, taking a job, being promoted to a position of greater responsibility) and *role deficits* (getting divorced, retiring, being widowed). Not all changes in circumstances involve major role changes, to be sure. One may make a residential move or a horizontal job move, for instance, without taking on new roles or shedding old ones. But many events of adult life do entail either a role gain or a role loss.

Can all the changes in adult life, all the turning points that people experience, be equated with crisis? Most authorities seem to believe that they cannot. For instance, Neugarten (1976) maintains that the expected change, the change that occurs "on time" and for which the individual has "rehearsed," is not particularly traumatic:

> The end of formal schooling, leaving the parents' home, marriage, parenthood, occupational achievement, one's own children growing up and leaving, menopause, grandparenthood, retirement—in our society, these are normal turning points, the markers or the punctuation marks along the life cycle. They call forth changes in self-concept and in sense of identity, they mark the incorporation of new social roles, and accordingly, they are the precipitants of new adaptations. But in themselves they are not, for the vast group of normal persons, traumatic events or crises that trigger mental illness or destroy the continuity of the self [p. 18].

As we have seen, Neugarten also believes that the nonoccurrence of an event may constitute a crisis: the young man who graduates from college and then is unable to find a suitable job, the young woman who is not married as she approaches her late 20s, the middle-aged adult who has not advanced up the career ladder at the expected pace—these people may suffer negative feelings from being "off time."

Levinson, Darrow, Klein, Levinson, and McKee (1976) point out that transitions may be made quietly and without turmoil. Clausen (1972) says that some people go through a transition period without even being aware of it. Brim (1977) states: "The concept of 'crisis' implies a rapid or substantial change in personality, and it is probably both rapid and substantial rather than either one alone, which is dislocating with respect to one's sense of identity" (p. 6).*

But perhaps the question is purely academic. Presumably, counselors of adults will be dealing with people who are not making a transition smoothly, who are experiencing confusion, discontent, and other negative feelings as they try to cope with change in their lives, who seek out help to get them over the rough spots. Perhaps a more fruitful concept, from the standpoint of the counselor, is that of stress.

Stress

Any life event that brings about changes (Lowenthal, Thurnher, Chiriboga, & Associates, 1975) and that requires adjustment on the part of the individual (Holmes & Rahe, 1967) constitutes a *stress*. A stress can be positive—eliciting exuberance, excitement, an increase in life satisfaction—as well as negative. Whatever the direction of the impact, however, stress exacts a toll on the person experiencing it. Holmes and Rahe have developed a Social Adjustment Rating Scale (see Chapter 7 for a copy of this instrument) in which numerical values are assigned to different kinds of life changes. "Death of a spouse" ranks at the top of the scale as the most severe stress that a person can experience; such items as "vacation," "Christmas," and "minor violations of the law" are at the bottom of the scale. A person's total score for a given year is supposedly related to his/her physical and mental health. Even the person who is gifted at coping with stress may require outside help if heavily overloaded with stressful events during a relatively short period. Not only do people differ from one another in coping

strength (because of inherent ability, learning through experience, or a combination of the two), but also the same person may react differently to a particular event depending on when it occurs in the life span. As Neugarten (1976) puts it:

> Major stresses are caused by events that upset the sequence and rhythm of the life cycle—as when death of a parent comes in childhood rather than in middle age; when marriage does not come at its desired or appropriate time; when the birth of a child is too early or too late; when occupational achievement is delayed; when the empty nest, grandparenthood, retirement, major illness, or widowhood occur off-time [p. 20].

The importance of the timing of a particular life event is illustrated by the following true story of two women, both of whose husbands had undergone open heart surgery during the previous year. As they compared notes, it became obvious that their reactions were very different. The first woman seemed outraged that fate should have played such a trick on her and irritated at her husband for his depression following the operation. The second woman, though very upset at the time of the surgery, was delighted that her husband's health problem had been resolved. This difference in reaction is probably attributable to the difference in life stage of the two couples. The first woman was 32, her husband 35. She had barely begun her career training, he was working his way up through the bureaucratic structure but had not yet arrived at the top. To her, the heart surgery represented a sudden limitation imposed on their aspirations. The second couple was 20 years older. Both husband and wife were pursuing careers that interested them and had, indeed, achieved many of their occupational goals. The wife saw the heart surgery as a reprieve from widowhood, the husband as an additional 20 years of life. Both couples experienced a life-and-death trauma; each interpreted it differently.

Examining perceived stress across the life cycle, Beeson and Lowenthal (1975) found both

*From "Theories of the Male Mid-Life Crisis," by O. G. Brim, Jr. In N. K. Schlossberg and A. D. Entine (Eds.), *Counseling Adults*. © 1977 by Wadsworth Publishing Company, Inc. This and all other quotations from this source are reprinted by permission of the publisher, Brooks/Cole Publishing Company.

life-stage and sex differences. Younger subjects reported more stresses during the previous 10 years than did older subjects, an indication that the tempo of life tends to slow down as one gets older. Newlyweds of both sexes, and men in the preretirement stage, reported more positive than negative stresses; middle-aged couples of both sexes, and women in the preretirement stage, reported more negative than positive stresses. The source of stress varied among the different groups, with sex differences being particularly marked among the older adults. Work was the primary source of stress for men, reported by half of the middle-aged group and one-third of the preretirement group. The most striking characteristic of older women was their tendency to regard as stressful the changes that occurred in the lives of others close to them. Thus, they were more deeply concerned with their husbands' work and health and with events in the lives of their children than they were with changes in their own lives.

The following stress typology (Lowenthal & Chiriboga, 1975, p. 147) is based on two dimensions: (1) exposure to stress, as indicated by factual reports of the subjects (a modification of the Holmes/Rahe scale was used to measure severity of stress); and (2) preoccupation with stress, as indicated by the tendency of the subjects to dwell on stressful events when talking about their lives. Four types may be defined on the basis of response to stress:

STRESS TYPOLOGY*

	Preoccupation with Stress	
Presumed Stress	Thematic in presentation	Not thematic
Frequent and/or severe	Overwhelmed	Challenged
Infrequent and/or mild	Self-defeating	Lucky

*From *Four Stages of Life: A Comparative Study of*

Generally, the more educated the individual, the more likely he or she is to have varied life experiences and thus to be exposed to more stresses. Again, life-stage and sex differences were found: Of the highly stressed, more men than women in the two younger groups, but more women than men in the two older groups, belonged to the "overwhelmed" rather than the "challenged" category. Of the lightly stressed, older men and women and younger men were more likely to be "lucky," and younger women were more likely to be "self-defeating."

In addition, the "lucky" were distinguished from the "self-defeating" by their intrapersonal characteristics; they emerged as being somewhat shallow, avoiding involvement with other people, distancing themselves from life, expressing little emotion. The "self-defeating" were preoccupied with the past and with death and had a negative self-image. The younger adults among them often expressed feelings of isolation because of their national or ethnic origins; the middle-aged women among them were depressed over their poor marriages.

Interpersonal, as opposed to intrapersonal, characteristics differentiated between the "challenged" and the "overwhelmed." The former were more likely to have close and trusting relations with others, whereas the latter tended to rate themselves low in capacity for intimacy. Many of those in the "overwhelmed" category had suffered childhood deprivation—such as the loss of a parent through death or divorce—a finding that gives substance to Neugarten's contention that the off-time event is more traumatic than the expected event. Of those subjects who reported such a loss, younger

Women and Men Facing Transitions, by M. F. Lowenthal, M. Thurnher, D. Chiriboga, and Associates. Copyright 1975 by Jossey-Bass, Inc. This and all other quotations from this source are reprinted by permission.

adults of both sexes and older women—but not older men—were more likely to belong to the "overwhelmed" category. Lowenthal and Chiriboga (1975) offer the following explanation for this sex difference: "These men, in comparison with their female cohorts, were (through their work involvements and other commitments outside the home) exposed to more ego-strengthening experiences, which served as buffers against the continuing effect of early losses" (p. 158).

Stock-Taking

Periodically as people move through life, and especially as they approach transitions that may involve changes in life structure or role transformations, they pause to take stock of themselves: their dreams, their achievements, their options. Often this reassessment leads to the difficult realization that one has not lived up to earlier expectations and aspirations. The earlier goal—of becoming a noted writer, a famous scientist, an influential statesman —bumps up against the hard reality that one has gone as far as possible and has fallen short of the mark set in younger days. According to Brim (1976):

> Over the course of the working life, from entry to the mid-life period, it is likely that although aspirations may be adjusted downward on occasion, one usually believes there is enough time left for the desired level of achievement to be reached in future years. But during mid-life most American males must adjust their career aspirations of earlier years downward to fit current reality. A man may be told that he has risen as high as he can go in his place of work; that his present position must be accepted by him as the achievement level for his lifetime [p. 5].

Even people who are relatively successful in achieving the goals they earlier set for themselves may experience a sense of disparity between what they have and what they want. According to

Levinson et al. (1977): "Many men . . . enter adulthood with a Dream or vision of their own future. . . . Major shifts in life direction at subsequent ages are often occasioned by a reactivation of the sense of betrayal or compromise of the Dream" (p. 52).* Women, too, may experience a sense of loss as their options are narrowed, their potentialities go unrealized, and their desire for completeness is thwarted. Lowenthal et al. (1975) found that the middle-aged women in the San Francisco study were often desperate: having led family-centered lives, the prospect of the empty nest was very upsetting to them. Many "expressed a desire for personal growth, a wish to break out of the family confines, though they could envisage few realistic possibilities for doing so" (pp. 235-236).

The notion of "mid-life crisis" has been popularized by the mass media, but experts disagree about just when it occurs—whether in the 30s, the 40s, the 50s, or even later. For example, Levinson et al. (1976) identify both an "Age 30 Transition" and a "Mid-Life Transition"; the latter usually begins around age 38 and peaks in the early 40s. Both periods "may occasion considerable turmoil, confusion, and struggle with the environment and within oneself" (p. 23).

Erik Erikson (1950) describes a sequence of crises in adult life following resolution of the adolescent crisis of ego identity. In his terms, the mid-life crises are *generativity* (the sense of having contributed to future generations, either through one's own offspring or through creation and productivity in the arts, science, and so forth) and *ego integrity* (the acceptance of one's own life as meaningful and

*From "Periods in the Adult Development of Men: Ages 18 to 45," by D. J. Levinson, C. M. Darrow, E. B. Klein, M. H. Levinson, and B. McKee. In N. K. Schlossberg and A. D. Entine (Eds.), *Counseling Adults.* © 1977 by Wadsworth Publishing Company, Inc. This and all other quotations from this source are reprinted by permission of the publisher, Brooks/Cole Publishing Company.

right). Failure to resolve the first of these two crises produces feelings of stagnation, worthlessness, and personal impoverishment; failure to resolve the second results in feelings of despair and a fear of death.

In the San Francisco study, Lowenthal and Pierce (1975) found that middle-aged parents were in many ways the most discontented of the four "pretransitional groups" analyzed. The men were often bored with their jobs and uneasy about the future; they looked forward to retirement with anxiety. The women were extremely unhappy, although they were less able to pinpoint the cause; they complained frequently of marital problems, of concern over the health of their husbands, of worry about their children, and of frustration over the lack of opportunities for personal growth. The oldest group—preretirement couples—were more satisfied with their lives and less distressed generally. But all four groups (high school seniors, newlyweds, middle-aged parents, preretirees) experienced some problems as they sought to adjust to new demands and adopt new roles.

The term *middlescence* has been used to describe the mid-life crisis, but perhaps it is more appropriate to talk about a series of "middlescences," each involving a reassessment of one's life and one's self and a consequent decision about where to go next. The crisis accompanying the empty nest need be no more memorable than the crisis of becoming a parent for the first time. LeMasters (1957) found that the birth of the first child was a pivotal event to most parents, accompanied by anxiety, ambivalence, and in some cases extreme depression.

Although adults of any age may go through a crisis that involves reassessment, the stock-taking of middle age is characterized by an increased "interiority," or focus on the inner self, a concern with self-utilization, and a reevaluation of competency. This last process is heightened for people in the middle generation of their families. They see their children as being more competent than they in the enjoyment of sex, of love, of life. At the same time, they see their parents on the decline. The comparison of the older with the younger generation adds to their own sense of loss, increases their fear of aging, and reconfirms the feeling that their mastery of self and environment is on the decline.

A somewhat more sanguine view of the middle years is given by Neugarten (1968). Interviewing 100 "well-placed" men and women in the 40–60 age group, she found a "heightened sensitivity to one's position within a complex social environment," a "willingness to explore the various issues and themes of middle age," and a conviction "that middle adulthood is the period of maximum capacity and ability to handle a highly complex environment and a highly differentiated self" (pp. 93–97). These people saw themselves as the bridge between generations. Although they felt an increasing distance from the young—and in many cases were concerned with "acting their age"—they also had a greater empathy with older people. Sex differences were marked. The women emphasized their greater freedom: "Not only is there increased time and energy now available for the self, but also a satisfying change in self-concept. . . .Middle age marks the beginning of a period in which latent talents and capacities can be put to use in new directions" (p. 96). In contrast, the men often suffered heavy job pressures or job boredom. Nonetheless, both sexes reported an increased sense of competence, a greater self-understanding, a confidence in their expertise. In short, they seemed to deserve the title bestowed upon them by *Time* magazine: "the Command Generation."

Thus, the stock-taking that usually accompanies transition may produce in some people a renewed self-confidence at having triumphed over difficulty and gained new coping strength. But others—trapped in current anxieties or panic and longing for change, excitement, and self-fulfillment

—may make hasty decisions and employ desperate stratagems to escape. Still others may be so fearful of change that they become immobilized, unable to act, sinking deeper and deeper into depression. The desperation and the depression are intensified by feelings of isolation. As Levinson et al. (1976) point out:

> A myth supported by most theories of pre-adult development is that at the end of adolescence you get yourself together and, as a normal, mature adult, you enter into a relatively stable, integrated life pattern that can continue more or less indefinitely. This is a rather cruel illusion since it leads people in early adulthood to believe that they are, or should be, fully adult and settled, and that there are no major crises or developmental changes ahead [p. 23].

The discovery that life is not going as smoothly as expected may lead many adults to feel that they are in some way deviant, abnormal, unique. They may not be aware that other adults face the same problems and experience the same self-doubts, regrets for lost hopes, and feelings of inadequacy. One of the most important services that the counselor can perform for adult clients is to assure them that they are not alone, that other people share the same experiences, that they are in the statistical sense "normal."

Shift in Time Perspective

One of the most dramatic interior events that occurs during adulthood is a shift in time perspective, when one starts thinking in terms of time-left-to-live rather than time-since-birth. Neugarten (1968) believes that this shift is somewhat more important for men than for women. Men become more aware of the loss of strength and vigor, more concerned with their health, more fearful that time is running out for them. As one of the "well-placed" men interviewed by Neugarten (1968) expressed it:

> Time is now a two-edged sword. To some of my friends, it acts as a prod; to others, a brake. It adds a certain anxiety, but I must also say it adds a certain zest in seeing how much pleasure can still be obtained, how many good years one can still arrange, how many new activities can be undertaken [p. 97].

Women, on the other hand, become more concerned with the health of their loved ones, particularly their husbands; they may "rehearse for widowhood" (Neugarten, 1968, p. 97). Nonetheless, they, too, may be overwhelmed with the awareness that they have little time left.

Another aspect of the shift in time perspective is a confrontation with death. Death becomes personalized, no longer something that happens to other people. Lowenthal and her associates (1975) found that thoughts of death were not necessarily more frequent among older subjects than among younger ones, but that the circumstances giving rise to such thoughts varied by stage:

> Older people thought of death mainly in connection with specific and personal circumstances, such as the death of a friend; younger people were likely to have death thoughts in response to general events such as accidents, earthquakes, or wars. Marriage, and especially parenthood, was reported to evoke thoughts about death which transcend the self, the concern being for the survivors [p. 299].

To Brim (1976), "one of the major psychological tasks for middle age is resignation to death and a permutation, a reordering of life priorities" (p. 6). If this task is accomplished successfully, the result may be a release of new energy; if not, the result may be the despair that Erikson discusses.

Although most experts talk about the change in time perspective as occurring in middle age, it can actually take place at any point in the life cycle where one perceives one's options as narrowing. For instance, recently one of the authors talked with three different adults, all of whom expressed concern about time. One, a man of 58, was highly successful in business but did not enjoy his work. He suddenly realized that if he did not make an immediate change, he would never again have the chance to do so. His realization may be contrasted with that of a young man of 33 who had moved up the career ladder very rapidly, publishing articles and books and being recognized as an authority in his field. Nevertheless, he felt that fewer jobs were now available to him and that he might end up in a rut. Eight years before, when he was just starting his career, he had had ten different job offers, but this year, only two. The third person, a woman of 46, was ready to emerge from her previous status of full-time homemaker but was unsure of just what she wanted to do with the rest of her life. She kept saying "I want to apply to some program, any program, right away." All three adults were haunted by the conviction that time was running out on them.

Locus of Control

The concept of control is central to all areas of an individual's life: work, family, friendship, community. Julian Rotter (1966) hypothesizes that a person's "locus of control" determines the way that person shapes his or her life. The locus of control can be either internal or external. People with an internal locus of control perceive themselves as having power over their own destiny; they believe that what they do makes a difference in what happens to them. They are actively involved in making decisions about jobs as well as about other events in their lives. At the other extreme, people with an external locus of control feel like puppets on a string; they believe they are controlled by other people, by impersonal social forces, or by fate. Thus, they are passive, apathetic, unwilling to make decisions because they feel that such decisions are irrelevant to what happens to them.

The feeling of helplessness associated with an external locus of control is related to profound psychological discomfort, even to severe illness and death. Laboratory animals, and human beings, have been known to die from no observable physiological cause when they find themselves in situations where they feel completely helpless. Not only such "psychosomatic" disorders as hypertension, asthma, and colitis, but even leukemia, malignant tumors, and infectious diseases may be related to severe stress accompanied by hopelessness. There appears to be a "giving up" complex (Colligan, 1975).

In the San Francisco study (Lowenthal & Pierce, 1975), it was found that women generally had less sense of being in control of their lives than did men, that younger people were only slightly more likely to feel themselves in control than were older ones, and that middle-aged parents were most likely of all four groups to experience helplessness. The authors conclude: "The sense of inner control was clearly the most important of the pretransitional conditions, being strongly associated with a positive attitude toward the transition, as well as with planning for it" (p. 209).

Clearly, then, a primary goal in counseling adults is to intervene in ways that enable clients to take control, and to feel in control, of their lives. The counselor's task is not to move people in particular directions or to discourage them from particular courses of action but to help them develop strategies that they can apply in considering options and making decisions.

REPRESENTATIVE THEORISTS

Another way of organizing material on adulthood is by looking at the work of some representative theorists. The summaries presented here are necessarily brief and by no means intended to convey the full range of that theorist's thought. The individuals whose work is discussed were selected primarily because they represent different approaches to development in later life. Many other writers have also made significant contributions to the body of knowledge about adult development. Among those who should be mentioned is Brim (1976), who presents a sociological view and emphasizes the importance of major life events. Riley, Johnson, and Foner (1968) have elaborated an age-stratification theory that considers the combined effects of individual aging, cohort membership, and historical period. Gould (1972) has proposed a theory of psychological development based upon clinical interviews over time.

Many of the theorists whose ideas are discussed more thoroughly in the following section can be classed as "stage" theorists. At this point in the study of adult development, stage theories seem to be most appealing because of their relative simplicity; as our knowledge advances, "open-ended" theories—capable of greater elaboration—may become more prominent.

Havighurst

A stage theory involving developmental tasks is proposed by Robert Havighurst (1953). Each period or stage of life calls for the solution or completion of a set of tasks, the success of which is related to life satisfaction in that period. The tasks required in early adulthood are: selecting a mate, learning to live with that mate, starting a family, rearing children, managing a home, getting started in an occupation, taking on civic responsibility, and finding a congenial social group. In later adulthood, one has to accomplish the following tasks: achieving civic and social responsibility, establishing and maintaining an economic standard of living, assisting teenage children to become responsible and happy adults, engaging in appropriate leisure activ-

ities, relating oneself to one's spouse as a person, accepting and adjusting to the physiological changes of middle age, adjusting to aging parents.

Havighurst holds these developmental tasks to be universal, necessary, and desirable. One must complete these tasks if one is to be a "good adult." The counselor's functions, then, are to see to it that clients are dealing with the tasks appropriate to their time of life and, perhaps, to tell them the right ways of dealing with them.

Erikson

Erik Erikson (1950) proposes an eight-stage progression in ego development over the whole life span. Each stage is characterized by a different crucial issue that is either resolved successfully or not; failure to achieve a successful resolution at one stage impedes all later development. The first four stages belong to infancy and childhood. The last four stages, starting in early adolescence, are: identity (versus role diffusion), intimacy (versus isolation), generativity (versus stagnation), and ego integrity (versus despair).

Thus, the main crisis of adolescence is that of establishing ego identity—a sense of knowing who you are, a sense of belonging. Young people who fail to achieve a sense of identity are left with role diffusion and are unable to progress further; those who do establish a clear identity are ready to go on to the next stage of forming a true close relationship with another person. Failure to do this results in feelings of isolation and loneliness. Should one be successful in establishing intimacy, one proceeds to the issue of generativity: expanding one's interests; creating new people, products, or ideas; contributing to society. Failure to achieve generativity leads to a feeling of stagnation. One does not usually arrive at the final stage—ego integrity—until late adulthood, when one looks back over one's life and decides whether it has been worth living. Failure to find meaning in life results in despair and fear of death.

In an empirical study of over 100 men and women between the ages of 40 and 65, Gruen (1964) translated Erikson's theoretical formulations into behavioral terms. He found that the individual's stage of development was not related to chronological age, sex, or social class, but the concept of sequentiality did receive some substantiation. For instance, people scoring low on identity were also likely to score low on intimacy.

The counselor following Erikson's theory would search for ways to help clients deal with the particular crucial issues they were facing. For instance, if the client were undergoing a crisis involving intimacy—a failure to establish a close relationship with another person—the counselor would first try to ascertain whether the client had succeeded in establishing identity; if not, the counselor would focus on that issue first, before going on to help the client overcome feelings of isolation.

Kohlberg

The focus is on moral development rather than ego development in the theory of Lawrence Kohlberg (1973). He sees people as moving through various stages of moral judgment, based on their understanding of the right way to behave toward other people and toward society in general.

During late childhood and adolescence, as the individual develops intellectually, progressing from simple to more complex cognitive processes, he or she is also likely to become more complex in moral attitudes. But only the adult can reach the highest stages. The progression of moral-judgment stages goes from preconventional to conventional to post-conventional. Behavior at all three stages may be the same, but the motivation for it will differ. For instance, a person at the preconventional stage may behave honestly out of fear of being punished for dishonesty; a person at the conventional stage may behave honestly because of a feeling that it is the "thing to do"; and a person at the postconventional stage may behave honestly because he/she has weighed the value and meaning of honesty and is committed to the principle.

Counseling based on Kohlberg's paradigm would be aimed at helping clients move from a low level to the next higher level of moral judgment by confronting them with moral dilemmas that would lead them to reevaluate their behavior.

Loevinger

The theory of development proposed by Jane Loevinger (1976) bears many resemblances both to Kohlberg's and to Erikson's. Her emphasis, however, is on ego control, which includes the areas of interpersonal relations, moral judgment, and conceptual complexity. Thus, moving from lower to higher levels, one can classify people as impulsive (out of control, intolerant), self-protective, conformist, conscientious, autonomous, and integrated. A person at a lower level of ego development is not as open to complexity as a person who is at the autonomous or integrated stage. Thus, two clients with similar problems but at different levels would have to be helped differently: too many options would be confusing and upsetting for someone at the conformist stage; not enough options would be constricting and inappropriate for the client at the autonomous stage.

Unlike most stage theorists, Loevinger cautions against idealizing any stage. Thus, it is wrong to assume that a person at a higher stage of development is necessarily a "better" person than someone at a lower stage. In adapting any of these stage theories to practical use, the effective counselor would do well to bear this stricture in mind: a given theory may have value for organizing the counselor's thinking and for suggesting needed interventions, but attaching value labels to the various terms used by theorists is a disservice to the client.

Levinson

Based on an empirical study using the biographical method, the stage theory of Daniel Levinson and his associates (1976) focuses on relatively universal, age-linked periods in the lives of adult men. So far, they have defined five stages. (1) Leaving the family, which extends from late adolescence to ages 20–24, is a transition period during which the man is trying to develop independence from his family: he is half in and half out of the parental home. (2) Getting into the adult world, which occupies the early through the late 20s, begins after the man has established a new home base, is starting out in his occupation, and is attempting "to fashion an initial life structure" that links him with the wider adult world. (3) Settling down, a period that usually begins in the early 30s and extends to ages 39–41, has two rather conflicting aspects, one represented by order, stability, and commitment to career and family life, the other represented by mobility, upward striving, and ambition. (4) Becoming one's own man, which usually occurs in the middle to late 30s, is "the high point of early adulthood" (p. 23); typically, the individual feels that he is not independent and seeks to free himself from constraints. (5) The mid-life transition, which starts in the early 40s, resembles the earlier leaving-the-family stage in that it is a transitional period between two periods of relative stability; it may be a period of considerable turmoil as the man senses a disparity between what he is and what he wants to be.

This model of adult male development has gained widespread attention. It should be borne in mind, however, that the sample of men studied by Levinson and his associates is very small (40 subjects). The four occupational groups included business executives, academic biologists, novelists, and blue- and white-collar industrial workers.

Gutmann

On the basis of studies with the Thematic Apperception Test, David Gutmann (1970) has noted age-related changes in the relation between the self and the environment which might be considered shifts in locus of control. Young adulthood is typified by self-confidence and risk-taking; the mode is active mastery. From about ages 20 to 50, thought and action are directed outward; the environment is perceived as challenging, something to be manipulated in order to get what one wants. In the middle years, the mode is passive mastery; the focus is turned inward on one's own thoughts and feelings and away from what is perceived to be a complex and hostile environment. The third mode, magic mastery, involves distorting one's perceptions of the environment to reduce feelings of helplessness; old people are more likely than are younger people to convince themselves in this way that they will get what they want or have already attained it. In addition to the connection with age, the mode of mastery also varies by sex.

Lowenthal

Marjorie Fiske Lowenthal and her associates (Lowenthal et al., 1975), like Levinson, take an empirical approach to the study of change in the adult years. Using interviews with four different groups of men and women living in the San Francisco area, each at the onset of a major transitional period—high school seniors, newlyweds, middle-aged parents, and preretirement couples—they found that each group anticipated different life changes, faced different sources of stress, and had different ways of coping with that stress. Moreover, there were marked sex differences at each of these life stages. For instance, the two younger groups were much more likely than the two older groups to perceive education as a major source of stress, but younger women cited residential changes and dating/marriage as next most stressful, whereas younger men cited leisure activities and the military. Older men (especially the middle-aged) saw work-related issues as stressful, whereas older women were much more likely to cite family issues and health problems (usually the health of others, especially the husband, rather than their own health).

Various intrapersonal dimensions—such as time orientation, simplicity/complexity, self-concept—and their relation to adaptation through the life course were examined. One of the most significant and surprising findings to come out of this study is that psychic complexity was adaptive among the younger subjects but not among the older: the more complex the older person, the more likely he or she was to be unhappy with self and life. "The psychologically simplistic, who have sought and developed self-protective, stress-avoidant life styles, are likely to age most comfortably in our present culture. . . . This state of affairs . . . is not only a waste of human resources from a social point of view but threatens misery on the familial level as well" (Lowenthal et al., 1975, p. 243).

At this state of our knowledge, it is "highly premature" to adopt any global theory of adult development, according to Lowenthal. More research—particularly of a longitudinal and cross-sequential design—is needed to determine individual change over the life span as well as to investigate cohort differences brought about by sociohistorical changes.

Neugarten

Bernice Neugarten (1976)—some of whose ideas were discussed in Chapter 1—was one of the first life-cycle theorists to emphasize the influence of age-related life events and social expectations on individual development during the adult years. Neugarten specifies three different kinds of time: historical (or calendar) time, social time (or expectations), and life time (chronological age), all of which interact to produce the individual's life cycle.

Over the past century, historical trends have been such as to speed up the family cycle. People are marrying younger, having children sooner (and more closely spaced), and seeing their youngest child leave home earlier. Moreover, as the life span has increased, the postparental period has been extended considerably. At the same time, men are reaching economic maturity later than before, whereas women are entering the labor force sooner and middle-aged women are becoming more likely to return to the world of work. All these sociohistorical changes have profound effects on the rhythm of the individual life cycle.

In spite of these historical changes, however, people continue to be controlled by "social clocks":

> Because individuals live in contact with persons of all ages, they learn what to anticipate. There is a never-ending process of socialization by which the child learns what facets of his childhood behavior he must shed as he moves into adolescence; the adolescent learns what is expected of him as he moves from school to job to marriage to parenthood; and the middle-aged learn approved ways of growing old. Thus the social ordering of age-statuses and age-appropriate behavior will continue to provide a large measure of predictability [Neugarten, 1976, p. 17].

At the same time, certain inner changes take place as the result of adaptations over time both to biological and to social changes. People create more elaborate "mental filing systems": not only do they accumulate more information, but also they develop more "cross-references" on the basis of experience and of a more complete perception of the past.

According to Neugarten, it is the unexpected life event—not the normal, predictable one—that produces trauma. The man who has anticipated retirement at age 65 is not knocked off balance by this event; he has rehearsed for it and makes the change with equanimity. But the man who is suddenly forced to retire early, because he has had a heart attack or been fired, may suffer psychic damage. Similarly, the menopause and the empty nest are not as upsetting to middle-aged women as is commonly thought because they have been preparing for these events. Even death is faced with relative calm by old people; fear and unhappiness is generated by the prospect of dying in strange surroundings.

Like Lowenthal, Neugarten believes that it is presumptuous at this point to construct elaborate models of life-cycle development. All that can be done is to chart the kinds of behavior that tend to go with different age ranges, recognizing that these associations between age and behavior are themselves the product of the society in which they exist and are thus subject to change.

UNDERLYING ASSUMPTIONS

As can be seen from the above diversity of theories, adulthood can be viewed from several perspectives. Because our perspective as counselors determines, to a considerable extent, our attitudes toward and treatment of our adult clients, it is important that we recognize, clarify, and make explicit certain underlying assumptions of which we may not be conscious. For purposes of discussion, these assumptions are formulated as polarities: the static versus the dynamic view, inner versus outer determinants of change, open-ended versus stage development, and age-graded versus experiential determinants of change.

One's basic view of adulthood—as either static or dynamic—has important consequences for one's other orientations: for instance, the goals that the counselor has for the client, and the means that the counselor feels are appropriate for achieving these goals.

A focus on the *state* of being an adult implies that the adult years are stable. They may be seen as a time of responsibility, for example, or of power and knowledge. They may be seen as the end of the line. To take the static view involves asking such questions as: What are adults like as a group? What distinguishes them from children and adolescents at one end of the continuum and from the aging and aged at the other end? How should adultness be described? What is the right or the optimal way of being an adult? Are some people more adult or "mature" than others? Can the degree or quality of an individual's adultness be assessed? The counselor who takes the static view is concerned with helping clients achieve adultness by specifying the goals and characteristics of optimal adulthood and suggesting ways to reach or acquire them. Such an approach tends to be prescriptive; the counselor claims an insight into the "truth" about adultness and initiates rules and regulations for becoming adult.

As we stated at the beginning of this chapter, the static view was almost universal until very recently. Indeed, it is still widely accepted. Many schools of analysis and therapy assume that there is a "right" way of being an adult and that the client (or patient) must be helped to achieve that state. A key term is *adjustment*—adjustment to some absolute norm of adulthood.

On the other hand, a focus on the *process* of being an adult implies a more fluid definition of the adult years. They may be seen as a period of change, as the middle of life, not the end of the line. To take the dynamic view involves asking such questions as:

What makes adults change at all? Why do some people change (or develop), while others remain relatively the same through the years? In what ways are people likely to change, and when? Do people in their 20s differ systematically from people in their 30s, or 40s, or 50s? Do particular critical points or crises occur at certain times? Does one's coping ability improve as a reward for surviving over the years, or does the pressure of repeated stresses erode that ability? The counselor who takes the dynamic view may be concerned either with helping clients to change or with helping them to resist change and maintain stability. Whichever goal is chosen, the counselor will need to find which techniques work best to reach it.

As is obvious, the authors prefer to view adulthood as a process rather than a state, though both the static and the dynamic viewpoints may be useful to counselors of adults. If, then, we look at process, at development or at change, during the adult years, how do we understand this process?

Inner versus Outer Determinants of Change

For the early years of life, a biologically based maturational theory of development, though admittedly simple-minded, is at least credible; for the adult years, no such simple plan can be used. During childhood, biological changes are easy to see. Not only can they be measured in weeks and months rather than in decades, but also they are obviously related to other aspects of development, intellectual and social. It seems logical to believe that human beings are propelled by innate, biologically powered drives. After adolescence, however, biological changes slow down to the point of being almost imperceptible. Further, these biological events have little obvious connection with other aspects of adult behavior. Thus, the credibility of biologically based drives becomes weaker.

Nonetheless, some current theories of adult development resemble maturation theory in that they hold that there are inner "pushes" for certain kinds of behavior. For example, Abraham Maslow (1954) maintains that human beings have a drive for self-actualization: given the proper circumstances, people will strive for greater enhancement of their "potential." From this perspective, the counselor's task is to help people remove or overcome the barriers that may prevent them from self-actualizing. If the road ahead can be made free and clear, people will naturally want to follow it.

A variant of this theory is the competence theory of human growth and development, proposed by Robert White (1966). According to White, human beings of all ages have a persistent tendency to become more fit, more competent. This tendency is manifested in the child's propulsion toward continued exploration and manipulation of the environment. There is, White believes, a universal need to expand, explore, and achieve mastery over one's world and one's self. White differentiates between competence itself and its subjective aspect, the sense of competence, which is what we are talking about here. There are people, objectively competent in one or more areas such as academic study, who nonetheless feel themselves to be essentially incompetent. According to this perspective, the counselor's role is to assure clients that exploration is necessary for adults and to provide them with opportunities for new activities.

An opposite point of view holds that, because there are no biological pressures for change during the adult years, adults tend to remain stable and unchanging unless they are pushed into change by compelling outside events or social expectations. Only when they are shaken up by such common experiences as getting married, having a child, or getting a job—or when they feel it is time to do these things—will they go through any significant change. Thus, overpowering events produce the turning points in adult life. They can be accompanied by changes in life style and in social expectations. Whenever it is possible to anticipate these events, people tend to rehearse for them. Such rehearsing is more likely to occur in a stable society with well-defined expectations and clear models provided by older generations than it is in a rapidly changing society like our own. Most people create their own roles, and the experiences and behavior of their elders often seem irrelevant. From this perspective, the counselor's function is to encourage clients to anticipate future changes so that they can plan for them in advance. Presenting models to show them where and how to go is also useful. If change is deemed desirable in itself, it may even be deemed helpful to precipitate upsetting experiences.

Open-Ended versus Stage Development

Another way to view development is to see it as an open-ended process where what is to come next cannot be predicted. For example, Walter Mischel (1970) and others present a social-learning theory, which sees behavior as a product of past experience and the present situation. Change or development is particular to each individual and is tied to specific situations; it is not necessarily headed in any particular direction, nor need it follow any particular pattern. Though people may seem to go through similar stages, this similarity is explained by their sharing similar past experiences. From this perspective, the counselor's role is to help clients move in new directions by providing them with new and appropriate learning experiences.

A dialectical process is proposed by Klaus Riegel (1973), who sees development as moving from simple to complex through the progressive integration of previously inconsistent or contradictory experiences. Change occurs only when a person in an existing condition *(thesis)* is confronted by a conflicting or opposite situation *(antithesis)*. A successful resolution of this conflict would induce a higher-order new state *(synthesis)* which reconciles both elements of the conflict. This new synthesis becomes, in turn, the thesis to a new antithesis.

In contrast to open-ended theories are stage theories, which many counselors find useful for thinking about development. A variety of such theories have been suggested over the past century, though most of them assume that development ends at adolescence. The stage theories that do deal with adult development differ in a number of ways. For example, some hold that the stages they describe are universal, that everybody is bound to go through them in the same order at about the same time. Others view them as possibilities only: not everybody will go beyond the earlier stages, but a few people will go on to higher or later ones, and still other people have the potential to do so. Another way in which the theories differ is in their degree of normativeness. Some of them state that it is good or right to go through the sequence of stages in a particular way, or to move from one stage to the next at a particular age, and that it is bad to deviate from this pattern, whereas other theories do not make such evaluative statements.

Age-Grading versus Experiential Determinants

Another way to classify the various assumptions that underlie theories of adult development is in terms of their emphasis on age-grading. That is, some theories maintain that certain attitudes, behaviors, and problems are correlated with chronological age. Examples of highly age-graded models are those of Levinson and Havighurst. At the other extreme are the social-learning and dialectical theories discussed above, which emphasize the impact of each individual's unique experiences upon his or her present life situation. Neugarten, for instance, believes that the ubiquitous experiences of occupation and interpersonal relations are the cues for adult change. It is not being 40 years old that causes people to reevaluate their condition, but rather having been married for 20 years or being at the peak of their career or seeing their youngest child move out of the house, whatever the chronological age.

CHANGE IN ADULTHOOD: EMPIRICAL EVIDENCE

The preceding discussion has related to general themes of adult development. This section presents information gleaned from research on four major areas—physical, intellectual, personality, and sex-role. The effective counselor should remember, however, that individuals differ greatly in their rates of change, and that the generalizations presented here cannot be applied wholesale to particular clients.

Another caveat to bear in mind is that age changes are difficult to examine empirically because of methodological problems. Most research designs are cross-sectional—that is, different age groups are compared at a single point in time. The findings from such studies may tell us about age *differences,* but they say little about age *changes* in individuals. When the research is longitudinal and the same people are followed along over time, a different problem arises. Such research fails to take into account larger social and historical changes that may affect human beings, making one age cohort different from another. To take an obvious example: Early studies of scores on "omnibus" tests of general intelligence (IQ) found that young adults (ages 18–21) scored highest and that successive age groups scored progressively lower. This finding led researchers to conclude that intelligence deteriorates steadily and rapidly with age. But this conclusion overlooked the expansion in schooling that was taking place. Educational level is now known to correlate highly with IQ. Therefore, the lower IQ scores of older people are attributable not to declines in individual intelligence with age, but

rather to the younger subjects' having gone to school longer. Such secular trends may also account for differences in the values, interests, and even the physical condition of one generation and another. A methodological improvement would be a cross-sequential strategy (see Schaie, 1970). However, longitudinal and cross-sequential research is expensive and time-consuming, by its very nature, and thus may be less attractive to some researchers (and to the agencies that provide the funds for research, which often want fast results). Fortunately, several major longitudinal studies that started with children are now following them as adults.

Physical Development

Individual variation is the rule in physical development, and no physical change during adulthood can be exactly predicted from chronological age. The measure that correlates most highly is grayness of the hair (Fozard, Nuttal, & Waugh, 1972), and even on this relatively trivial physical characteristic, as we all know, people differ considerably. More generally, we all know people of 40 who seem very old, others who seem extremely youthful, and still others who seem to be just entering middle age.

Of the various factors that may account for individual differences with respect to physical change in the adult years, one of the most important is genetic endowment: longevity and long-lasting youthfulness run in families. Socioeconomic status (SES) is also related to physical development. People of lower SES tend to age faster and to die sooner than those from middle and upper levels; moreover, they generally suffer from poorer health throughout the life cycle. Some of these differences by socioeconomic level may be attributable to nutritional factors. Better nutrition also probably helps explain the slow trend, over the last 100 years, toward increases in height, weight, and longevity—although one must be cautious about asserting the value of a particular kind of diet, either for the individual or for groups of people. For instance, the Masai of Africa thrive on a diet of meat, milk, and blood, whereas people in neighboring tribes who follow essentially the same diet have higher cholesterol levels and a higher incidence of cardiovascular disease (Timiras, 1972). Exercise is another factor related to individual variations in physical change. Certain kinds of exercise seem to slow down physical aging, benefiting not only the large muscles but also the heart and brain. Finally, climate seems to be related to physical development, although it seems to affect different races differently. To complicate matters further, all these factors interact differently with one another and may have different effects on different people.

The relation between sex and physical development during adulthood is especially complex. Women, particularly middle-class women, tend to live longer and to remain youthful longer than do men. How much these differences are attributable to innate physiological differences and how much to differences in life style is not clear. Because our society puts a greater emphasis on youthfulness and physical attractiveness for women than for men, women may simply pay more attention to diet, exercise, cosmetics, and so forth. As another example of sociocultural influences, men are generally more susceptible to presumably stress-related physical disorders than are women; if a true sex revolution takes place and women come to participate in the world of work to the same extent and with the same degree of intensity as men do now, their incidence of stress-related disease may increase.

Various systems and functions of the body change at somewhat different rates. Thus, maximum height is attained at the beginning of adulthood, with no change thereafter. Around middle age, people have a tendency to put on weight, usually around the waist and hips. Strength peaks between ages 25 and 30, after which the muscles—particularly in the back and legs—weaken somewhat unless maintained by exercise. Manual dexterity is greatest at about age 33; then, the hands and fingers become progressively more clumsy. The senses dim as the years pass: The lens of the eye changes shape and becomes more opaque, resulting in far-sightedness. There is a gradual hearing loss after age 20, particularly among men. Sensitivity to smell decreases slightly at age 40, sensitivity to taste at age 50. However, the losses in all the senses are usually so small and so gradual that they are not noticed by most people until late middle age.

Appearance begins to alter at middle age. The hair starts to gray and to thin and the hairline to recede; the skin coarsens and darkens, especially around the eyes; wrinkles appear; changes in the teeth, bone, muscles, and connective tissue cause obvious changes in the lower part of the face. Because attractiveness is so central to the American woman's feeling about her worth, and because attractiveness is equated with youthfulness, these changes in appearance can dismay her. Similar changes, on the other hand, may make older men more attractive to young women as well as to older women (Nowak, 1974). There is a true "double standard of aging" so far as appearance is concerned (Sontag, 1972).

As a general rule, adults get fewer acute illnesses but more chronic illnesses than do children; they are less subject to respiratory infections and allergies but more prone to dental problems, high blood pressure, diabetes, arthritis, cardiovascular disorders, and digestive upsets. Moreover, older adults take longer to recuperate from illnesses and are less able to sustain great physical effort. Even though they do not have so many acute illnesses as the young, such illnesses can be more devastating.

Medical and dental visits become routine, and may become major items of the budget.

Sexual power appears to reach its peak in late adolescence for men and in the mid-20s for women (Masters & Johnson, 1966). Biologically, the relatively abrupt cessation of menses in women at some point during the 40s or 50s is significant because it means the end of fertility, though not of sexual activity or enjoyment. Male fertility declines more gradually and may not terminate for several decades beyond this time. Although there are hormonal changes in women, these changes seem to have only a minor effect on the personality and the mental health of well-functioning people. Several studies (for example, Neugarten & Kraines, 1965) have found that, whereas younger women tend to anticipate the menopause with anxiety, women actually going through it are much more concerned about their husband's health than their own and, in fact, are likely to perceive both this physiological milestone and the concurrent "empty nest" as liberating events.

These, then, are some of the major physical changes that take place in adulthood; the timing indicated is only general and approximate. Even before maturity, chronological age is an imperfect index of physical change. Child psychologists have tried to derive a developmental age, or functional age, that would more accurately indicate how far along a child is toward its mature level. Efforts are also being made to work out a developmental age for adults (Fozard et al., 1972). If these efforts succeed, it will become possible to estimate how far along adults are in their own life span. Distance from death may, in fact, be a more meaningful measure—though obviously harder to obtain—than distance from birth, particularly when one is concerned with the individual's options at a particular point.

Functional age can also be looked at psychologically, as the individual's perception of how old he or she looks, feels, thinks, and acts. One study (Kastenbaum, Derbin, Sabatini, & Artt, 1972) found that the "personal ages" of 60-year-olds deviated more from chronological age than did those of 20-year-olds and that appearance age was more closely related to chronological age than were the other "personal ages." In dealing with clients, counselors might give more consideration to the clients' own perceptions of their age identity.

Intellectual Development

Until very recently, it was thought that intellectual development followed an inverted U-shaped curve, ascending to a peak in the mid-20s and then declining; similarly, creativity or intellectual productivity was supposed to drop rapidly after middle adulthood. But the prospect is not quite so grim. Earlier studies of intelligence were usually cross-sectional, involving comparisons of younger and older adults at a single point in time and thus ignoring cohort differences, in particular the effects of longer schooling on intelligence. That more recent cohorts do better on standardized intelligence tests than did their predecessors is indicated by a steady rise in the "ceiling" age of intellectual growth as measured by the Stanford-Binet: from age 12 in 1917, to age 16 and then 21 up to 1957, and more recently to age 50 (Troll, 1975, p. 31). Longitudinal studies indicate that measured overall intelligence tends either to remain at a plateau or to increase slightly up to the last few years or months of life, then to drop drastically ("terminal drop"). Moreover, the higher a person's score is to begin with, the more likely that person is to maintain that score. In short, ability is related to stability in intelligence.

When intelligence is broken into components, it can be more easily understood. What Cattell

(1963) has called *fluid intelligence*—the capacity for rapid processing of information in problem-solving—declines steadily from the late teens. This capacity may depend on neural activity and speed of functioning. At the same time, however, *crystallized intelligence,* which relates to the storage of information such as vocabulary and general knowledge, increases over the adult years. Thus, the drop in fluid intelligence and the rise in crystallized intelligence tend to balance out, resulting in stability of general intelligence.

Changes in various aspects of intellectual functioning are consistent with these basic patterns. For instance, the individual tends to react more slowly with increasing age, but only when called upon to perform multiple trials in rapid succession. Long-term memory remains stable, especially if occasional practice is involved, though findings about short-term memory are contradictory. The higher mental processes of problem-solving, reasoning, and thinking may deteriorate slightly with age, at least when speed is called for. The effect of age on creative output varies with the product: mathematicians and physicists seem to produce their most original works during their 20s and 30s, but scientists and scholars whose work calls for accumulated knowledge and development do not reach their peak until much later in life.

Few studies have been done of the learning capacity of adults in the middle years, but the available evidence is congruent with what has already been said. When speed is called for, older subjects may not do so well: they are more likely to hesitate before responding, whereas younger subjects may plunge ahead, working by trial and error. To some extent, differences in learning ability may be related to differences in motivation. Older people may end up learning more—and learning it better—than younger people because the older people want more

intensely to learn and so work harder at it. For instance, most teachers in continuing education agree that people returning to education after a long absence make better students—more serious, dedicated, and hard working—than do "typical" undergraduates, the 18- to 21-year-olds.

What is important here from the standpoint of the counselor is that many popular notions about the effects of age on intellectual capability—as reflected, for instance, in the adage that you can't teach an old dog new tricks or in the belief that older people are forgetful—are seriously open to question. Moreover, in considering intelligence, the counselor should be aware that much more is involved than the ability to give quick answers or to make good grades. Wisdom, the accumulation of experience, the capability to cope with situations beyond the academic world—these are aspects of intelligence that should not be overlooked.

Personality Development

The term *personality* is difficult to define precisely, including as it does traits and attributes (which are supposedly "givens"), overt behavior, and attitudes, opinions, and feelings. Perhaps the most helpful concept of personality is that of a system—the integration of all behavioral elements into a whole, a "self" or an "ego." Theories of personality development in adulthood range from one extreme that emphasizes stability—institutionalization of the self early in life and its maintenance and protection against the buffets of life events—to the other extreme that sees the personality as unstable, fluctuating in response to the immediate situation. A third view sees the self-system as incorporating changes and thus being transformed into a new and different whole, even though it is still connected to the earlier self. Most people have a sense of continuing self. Whether this continuity is a matter of basic stability or of compensation to offset environmental pressures is impossible to say; it may differ for different people in different life circumstances.

In general, people who have coped well with early life stresses seem to be able to cope with those that come later. Women who have trouble with the menopause are likely to have had trouble with earlier psychosexual events such as puberty, sexuality, or childbearing, whereas those who have had no problems earlier tend to have no problems later. Generally, self-esteem seems to increase with the years. Although older adults may suffer more than younger ones from depression and anxiety, they seem to be less immobilized by it, better able to pick up their lives and go on. This difference, however, may represent a cohort effect rather than an improvement in the individual's coping skills over time. Obviously, it is important for the counselor to assess the amount of stress that clients are experiencing, as well as the way they have been able to handle past stresses, in order to estimate the amount of help they will need.

Thus, there is an evolving sense of self in response to changing life circumstances and continuing interactions between accumulated coping strategies and emergent stresses. At the same time, there is a set of persistent basic life values, combined with new experiences that either encourage or discourage, enhance or diminish, the expression of those values. For instance, interest in religion, religious belief, and church-going behaviors tend to remain relatively stable during the adult years, as do degree of unconventionality and general vocational interests. It is entirely possible, of course, that middle-aged adults will decide to pursue interests that were formed earlier but that they have previously suppressed or neglected for practical reasons. At least for men, achievement needs also seem to be stable. The middle-aged adult who strives for outstanding accomplishment in his or her occupation is usually the adolescent who sought to make all A's in high school.

Sex-Role Development

Men and women develop differently in our society, and in most other societies as well. Even in the area of physical development, as we have seen, some changes may be influenced by sociocultural rather than by physiological factors. In the area of intellectual development, research evidence indicates that women are generally superior in verbal ability and men in spatial and mathematical ability; that during adolescence the intellectual development of women, particularly of bright women, seems to slow down and even decline from previous levels, though in later years it may climb back up; and that women may have a "fear of success" (Horner, 1970) that leads them, consciously or unconsciously, to stifle their intellect.

Sex-role differences can also be talked about in Gutmann's (1970) terms, as described above. Young men see the world as a place they can mold or conquer: they are oriented to active mastery. Middle-aged men (for the middle class, roughly the 50s and 60s; for the working class, the 40s and 50s) see the world as more complex and dangerous and so become more concerned with their own thoughts and feelings: they become oriented to passive mastery. The pattern may be the reverse for women; that is, they may move over the adult years from a passive, dependent position to a stance of dealing more directly with the environment. Another way of expressing this idea is to say that women tend to become more *assertive* (less other-directed, more concerned with achievement, more driven by the need for power and self-actualization), whereas men become more *affiliative* (more nurturant, more concerned with their inner selves, more moved by a desire to form close personal ties) over the adult years.

These differences in the development of men and women are partly explained by differences in the socialization of the sexes. In our society, girls are inculcated with the "vicarious achievement ethic" (Lipman-Blumen, 1972); they learn early in life that women are supposed to define their identity through others—fathers, husbands, children, bosses. This ethic pervades not only their personal but also their occupational lives: even those who work outside the home usually hold lower-status, auxiliary positions—secretaries rather than executives, stewardesses rather than pilots, nurses rather than doctors—or work in "helping" professions such as teaching and social work. In contrast, early in their lives, males are locked into a direct achievement role; they learn as children that they must define their own identity and win their own successes. They are expected to work continuously, in order to provide for their families, and to shoulder the major responsibility of decision making.

In the middle years, however, both sexes may reach a turning point. Many women find that the pivots of their existence are gone. Their children have grown up and no longer need them; they may be widowed or divorced or simply isolated from their husbands by the years of leading separate existences. For their part, men may find that the world of work no longer holds the challenge or the promise that it once did: they have reached the peak of their careers (or have failed to do so and feel that they cannot go any further). It is not surprising, then, that at this point there can be a crossing-over of paths and an apparent reshuffling of roles. Looking back on their lives, both sexes may feel that they have missed out on something and thus may redirect their attention to the neglected areas: in the case of men, to human relationships, their own inner selves, the meaning of life; in the case of women, to achievement in the external world.

CONCLUSION

Optimally, change in the environment—as marked off by different life events that may or may not be traumatic—can lead to development. Much depends on the individual's degree of openness, on his or her ability to absorb and assimilate the input from the outside world. A system or a person is open if it lets in new experience or information; it is closed if it is insensitive or unresponsive, if it screens out or rejects new experience and information.

Human beings may respond to change in one of four ways. First, they may shut it out, denying the existence of anything that is new or that contradicts previous experience. We all know people who are so busy pretending that all is as it has been that they can no longer deal with reality: husbands or wives who do not see that their spouses have changed; athletes who refuse to acknowledge their waning physical prowess; parents who treat their grown-up children as though they were 6-year-olds.

A second response to change is to open up to it all the way, to seek new experience constantly. Carried to extremes, this solution leads to a total inability to cope, because coping requires controlling one's actions. In some instances, the system—or person—may even break down completely under the constant battery of new experiences.

A third response involves a minimal restoration of equilibrium. People may compensate for change just enough to return as closely as possible to a previous state of balance. For instance, a strongly family-centered woman may, when her youngest child leaves home, transfer all her affection and nurturing activities to another person, her husband perhaps, and treat him as though he were a child. The retired man may transfer all the energies that he previously devoted to a career to some hobby.

The fourth possible response is to grow and develop by incorporating the new experiences and information in such a way that the system itself is changed and the person becomes more complex.

At certain times in their lives, people are confronted with options or choices that are mutually contradictory: to choose one path is to reject another; to listen to one body of wisdom is to ignore another. Some control has to be exerted over the kind and amount of information that is taken in. The danger of being too open, too willing to absorb new experiences and to engage in new behaviors, is that the person may become fragmented. The counselor who is sensitive to this danger can guide clients in the direction of maintaining or increasing their control, rather than considering or trying to pursue every possible alternative. Recent divorcees and widows are particularly vulnerable. If they have been accustomed to making decisions jointly with their spouses, they may be unskilled at regulating their degree of openness to new possibilities for action and may find themselves out of their depth. The counselor can usually help in such cases, by aiding clients to develop a more firm and realistic self-definition and a clearer idea of what they want.

To summarize: If the turning points in life are to be the occasion for changes in life structure and in personality, two factors will determine the kinds of change that can result. One is the individual's degree of openness, and the other is the individual's degree of control over that openness. The two extremes—remaining completely closed and denying all change, or being completely open and absorbing more change than can reasonably be handled—both have unfavorable consequences. The human being must have good coping skills to be just open enough, to accept just the right amount of new experience, so that true development will result. The chief function of the counselor may be to see to it that the amount of new information or experience is adjusted to the skills of the client and to help the client control the amount of input.

For activities and skills related to this chapter, see Chapter 7.

3

Arenas in Which Adults Operate

According to Freud, the mature person is one who is able to love and to work. Erikson defines the two main developmental issues of the adult years as intimacy and generativity—again, love and work. In this chapter, we will look at these two main arenas in which adults operate. In the broadest sense, the arena of work includes not only paid employment, but also the education or training that serves as preparation for a job; but because of the complexity of the educational process—and because it is associated more with childhood and adolescence than with adulthood—the focus here is on occupation. The second arena is interpreted broadly to include various kinds of interpersonal relations, including friendships and family life.

WORK

In American society as it is presently structured, work is of prime significance in the lives of most adults. The kind of job that one has—or that some member of one's immediate family does—determines in large part the neighborhood in which one lives, the people one knows, the recreational activities that one engages in, the hours that one keeps.

The centrality of occupation is highlighted in the case of people who are fired from their jobs, or who are forced to retire at an earlier age than they would prefer, or who cannot get jobs in the first place. Being unemployed often results in discouragement, frustration, and loss of self-esteem. Some authorities question whether the majority of people can find satisfaction and self-fulfillment in the kinds of jobs available in a technological society, where the small family farm and business have been replaced by the giant bureaucratic organization and where the emphasis is on the efficient production of goods and services rather than on human development. Indeed, the trend toward part-time employment, a shorter work week, and earlier retirement—as well as toward lifelong education and the sharing of household and child-rearing duties by husband and wife—may well signal more fundamental changes. Nonetheless, at the present time, work still absorbs a major portion of the time and energies of most adults; and being employed is fundamental to their self-respect. Virtually all the adult men and almost half the adult women in the United States either have a job outside the home or are trying to find one. If we regard the role of homemaker as an occupation, then the participation of adults in the world of work becomes virtually total.

Varieties of Job Change

It is usually assumed that one chooses an occupation early in life—by the time one graduates from high school or in the undergraduate years—and is then locked into that choice until retirement. As a result, theories of vocational development have tended to focus on adolescence and early childhood. Their implication is that by about age 21, the die is cast: the basic decision has been made, and a person continues to develop only within that choice. Occupational distribution charts tend to illustrate this relationship between career choice and age. Clerical and service workers are younger; farmers tend to be aggregated in older age groups (Knox, 1977).

Despite the notion that the die is cast, job movement of some kind has long been accepted. A review of some of these types of changes follows. For example, people employed in bureaucratic organizations (probably no more than 30% of all workers) are expected to move steadily upward in the hierarchy from a low position at the time of entry to increasingly higher positions at appropriate intervals. Such movement constitutes an "orderly" career (Wilensky, 1961). Upward mobility is of two kinds: additive, involving a given number of years at each step in order to qualify for promotion to the next step (as in the army or civil service); and transformational, involving qualitative change, increases in expertise, wisdom, or managerial ability (as in academia, where one advances through the ranks from instructor to full professor, supposedly on the basis of increases in teaching ability and scholarship; or in various craft occupations of the past, where people advanced in rank from apprentice to master). There are certain expectations as to appropriate timing, and if a person is not promoted more or less on schedule, the result is frustration and a sense of failure. In such cases, the nonoccurrence of an expected event may constitute a stress. The feeling that one has advanced as far as one is going to get—but not as far as one had hoped and planned—may be an important causal factor in mid-life crisis.

In addition to upward movement within a status hierarchy, a fair amount of horizontal occupational mobility is characteristic of our society. Sometimes, this horizontal movement may take place within the same organization, as when the individual is moved from one department or office to another without any real change in position; this pattern may be more typical of women than of men, as when a secretary changes bosses. In addition, people may move from one employer to another. For instance, the unskilled worker may move from one factory to another within the same industry. A man with a Ph.D. in physics may take his first job at a college, then go to work in private industry, and then join a nonprofit research organization; or he may move from one academic institution to another. A national study of the American labor force between 1966 and 1969 (Parnes, Nestel, & Andrisani, 1972) found that one-fifth of those men who were employed in 1966 had changed employers by 1969. Over three-fifths of these changes were voluntary.

Such changes are more frequent in the early years on a job and thus among younger workers. Those who have had a job less than 5 years are seven times more likely to change than those who have had the same job for 20 years or more (Parnes et al., 1972). One of the reasons that older workers are less likely to change jobs is that they have an accumulated investment in their jobs—seniority and pensions. The investment is not merely financial, however. Becker and Strauss (1956) point out that the longer people remain in the same job, the more likely they are to become part of a cohesive job culture. Loyalty to a network of co-workers may work against job change.

A study of three generations of Minneapolis families (Hill, Foote, Aldous, Carlson, & Macdonald, 1970) revealed an increase in job mobility from the oldest generation (elderly grandparents at the time of the study) to the youngest (young adults), three in five of whom changed jobs during the year of observation. This increase in mobility was associated with a general rise in affluence (as measured by, for example, home ownership and acquisition of durable goods). Not only had the grandparent generation been poorer when they were younger, but also they were more likely to have been farmers than were either their children or their grandchildren; thus, they had been more tied to their jobs and had had little opportunity to look for other work. The grandfather, who had typically been married at about age 25, had in most cases still been working at his first job more than 5 years after that, when he was 30. In contrast, about half the grandsons, who usually got married several years younger, were in their second job by their second year of marriage, and 40% were in at least their fourth job by the time they had been married 10 years, when they were little more than 30 years of age.

Among the women in the three-generation study, labor force participation increased with each generation. Not until the postparental period (usually after 20 or more years of marriage) had as many as 20% of the grandmothers been employed outside the home. But 20% of their daughters (the middle-aged generation) had worked before marriage, only half had dropped out for childbearing and early child care, and most of them had returned to work before the end of 10 years of marriage. By the postparental period, almost half were employed, compared with one-fifth of their mothers. Though the granddaughters were still young at the time of the study, it seemed clear that this generational trend was continuing. Over three in five had been employed before getting married at a relatively early age. Although many were not working after 5 years of marriage (the childbearing period), many others were; and more had returned to work before they had been married 10 years. In other words, they spent fewer years at home raising their children.

The increase in job mobility over the three generations was related not only to greater affluence but also to prosperity; that is, people were more likely to make job changes when times were good. The importance of general economic conditions in influencing job change should not be underestimated. Recent surveys suggest that when the job market is tight, people are less willing to make changes, however dissatisfied they may be with their current jobs.

But some job changes are forced on people. Rapid technological advances have resulted in drastic changes in the world of work; specialization multiplies the types of jobs available but also renders them quickly obsolete. Alvin Toffler (1970) cites a survey by *Fortune* magazine that found that, of 1003 young executives in major corporations, one-third were employed in jobs that had not even existed until they stepped into them; another large proportion held jobs in which only one person had preceded them. The most startling increases in job turnover are occurring in the high-level professional, technical, and managerial occupations, though the highest rates of turnover are still found among the least skilled workers. When jobs become obsolete and workers are displaced, they have one of two choices: either they can retire early, or they can prepare for new careers. Toffler (1970) foresees a time when people will think in terms of "serial" careers, but so far that tendency is not widespread. We have been socialized into thinking that one should choose a career early and stick with it. Belbin and Belbin (1968) found it difficult to recruit workers for retraining programs; most preferred to accept downgrading rather than to retrain for new jobs.

Nonetheless, Toffler's forecast may not be too far off the mark. Major job changes from one field to another are becoming somewhat more widely accepted. Community colleges and proprietary schools offering vocational programs for adults have proliferated in recent years. Mid-life career change, especially among men who have been successful in relatively high-status jobs but who are discontent, has received considerable attention from the media. Empirical studies of such major change are, however, rare; and the few that do exist are limited in scope and sample size. They include investigations of teachers in the process of becoming counselors (Bingham, 1966), of men and women in the Boston area (Roe & Baruch, 1964), and of working-class men enrolled as undergraduates (Schlossberg, 1972).

But this paucity of data should not be taken to mean that such change is limited to the most exceptional and determined individuals. The following statements, made by people participating in a conference in career change sponsored by Wayne State University in 1965, indicate the range of people involved.

The Bus Driver. Well, I'm 30, Black, and male, and I've been driving buses for 13 years. About three years ago, I decided to become a sociologist . . . so now I'm taking undergraduate courses. The bus company cooperates with me in no way but to give me a bus. I drive the bus, and I don't want to cause any ripples. This is not the level I'm capable of performing. I threw away quite a bit of time because I had a chance to go to college on the G.I. bill, but at that time I never considered college. All I wanted to do was to get into something where my present abilities would suffice. . . . Another bus driver has a situation similar to mine. We are the same age. . . . He kept saying, "It's too late now, I'm 37." I'm not that much younger, but I don't feel too old.

The Insurance Salesman. I had some friends that were in the insurance business. They urged me to get in because of my sales ability. At that time, I was more interested in money than anything else. I was also active with alumni work, and when I was elected president of our Flint alumni group, I had some real misgivings. Since I had never graduated, I mean, this really bothered me. . . . I didn't want anyone to find out I hadn't graduated, so I decided to go back. . . . I got kidded good about college, when they said, "We've got a schoolboy with us." At age 42, I sold my business, then finished school, became a teacher, and am now a principal of an elementary school. . . . It was a great thing to me when the newspaper had a big article and picture about my being made principal.

The Homemaker. I remember the morning well. It was about 10 o'clock. All the children were in school, the house was straightened up, the dog and cat fed, and my husband out of town on a business trip. I was idly picking crab grass out of a scrubby lawn and feeling desperately bored. There was nothing to talk to my neighbors about, nothing I felt like doing in the house. I yearned for some intense involvement in something outside myself that had a goal. I wanted a job like I'd had before my first child was born and we moved to the suburbs. This feeling was so powerful that it overcame inertia. I made several telephone calls and wrote several letters, all within the space of an hour. I launched myself back to college to finish graduate work, to get my Ph.D., and to reenter the world of work.

What distinguishes people who are willing, or even anxious, to change jobs from those who are not? As was indicated, data are scarce, but one study (Sheppard & Belitsky, 1966) found that the former were more interested in the social-psychological characteristics of a job, had a stronger drive to achieve, and were dissatisfied with their present jobs, which they saw as providing few chances for upward mobility.

The question is: how much real change do all these job moves reflect? A way to analyze this is by examining the degree to which these changes occur between related areas. The classification system proposed by John Holland (1973), a relatively simple scheme though capable of great elaboration, can be used to classify both people (as personality types characterized by particular preferences, interests, and competencies) and environments (including groups of occupations). Each of the proposed categories is dominated by a given personality type and characterized by a physical setting that makes specific demands and provides specific opportunities. The six model environments (with examples of occupations in each) are:

1. Realistic (R): Involves "the explicit, ordered, or systematic manipulation of objects, tools, machines, and animals" (p. 29). (Examples of occupations are architectural draftsman, filling station attendant, watch repairman, structural steelworker, maid, railroad brakeman, miner, surveyor, fish and game warden.)
2. Investigative (I): Involves "the observation and symbolic, systematic, creative investigation of physical, biological, or cultural phenomena" (p. 30). (Examples of occupations are economist, physicist, medical technologist, surgeon, computer programmer, agronomist, aeronautical engineer, airplane navigator, mathematician.)
3. Artistic (A): Involves "ambiguous, free, unsystematized activities and competencies to create art forms or products" (p. 30). (Examples of occupations are drama coach, musician, entertainer, writer, designer, architect.)
4. Social (S): Involves "the manipulation of others to inform, train, develop, cure or enlighten" (p. 31). (Examples of occupations are interviewer, historian, counselor, physical education teach-

er, social worker, physical therapist, homemaker, clergyman.)
5. Enterprising (E): Involves "the manipulation of others to attain organizational or self-interest goals" (p. 32). (Examples of occupations are banker, lawyer, salesman, retail merchant, stewardess, radio/TV announcer.)
6. Conventional (C): Involves "the explicit ordered, systematic manipulation of data, such as keeping records, filing materials, reproducing materials, organizing written and numerical data according to a prescribed plan, operating business and data processing machines" (p. 33). (Examples of occupations are key punch operator, file clerk, certified public accountant, telegraph operator, library assistant.)*

Three-letter codes are used to describe more precisely both people and occupations. These codes indicate not only the primary area of interest or job aspect but also the secondary and tertiary areas. In addition, Holland uses another dimension, called level, to indicate the degree of education or training required for a particular occupation. For instance, the occupations of logger and mechanical engineer can both be coded RIE, but the former requires no more than an elementary school education, whereas the latter requires professional training. Holland states: "People search for environments that will let them exercise their skills and abilities, express their attitudes and problems, and take on agreeable problems and roles" (1973, p. 4).

Job Satisfaction and the Concept of Congruence

In Holland's view, vocational interests are a general expression of one's personality; similarly, Lowenthal (1972) sees job orientation as an aspect of lifestyle. Nonetheless, different people are

*From *Making Vocational Choices: A Theory of Careers,* by John L. Holland. © 1973. Adapted by permission of Prentice-Hall, Inc., Englewood Cliffs, New Jersey.

involved in their work to different degrees. Or, to put it another way, different people look for different kinds of rewards and satisfactions in their jobs.

Examining relationships between job satisfaction and various demographic factors, one study (Quinn, Staines, & McCullough, 1974) has found that younger workers tend to be more dissatisfied with their jobs than do older workers. This tendency may in part represent a generational effect. Reviewers of earlier findings (for example, Hurlock, 1968; Crites, 1969) have found that young people starting out on their first job were often exhilarated by the independence it gave them, even though the job itself was not intrinsically rewarding. The generational difference may reflect the upward shift in educational level. As more and more young people have gone on to college, their expectations about work may have changed. If these expectations are unfulfilled, their dissatisfaction may be sharper than that of an older generation. In addition, the youngest workers today are those who have not attended college (or, in some cases, even finished high school) and who are thus qualified only for low-level jobs.

Dissatisfaction tends to be greater among Blacks and other minority groups than among the White majority. Again, this may be attributable to the concentration of minority-group members in low-level jobs. Even though workers at all occupational levels are subject to dissatisfaction, it is most rampant among those at the lowest levels: factory operatives, nonfarm laborers, and those in low-status service occupations. Female workers do not differ significantly from males in this respect, but having preschool children makes for greater job dissatisfaction among both women and men.

Generally speaking, the higher the level of education, the more likely people are to be satisfied with their jobs. People with a high school education are more likely to be satisfied than are those with only a grade school education. College graduates are most likely to be satisfied with their jobs. Once again, the greatest dissatisfaction is likely to be found among those in low-level jobs—jobs that do not require a high school (or higher) education.

People at different job levels regard different aspects of their work as important (Quinn et al., 1974). Blue-collar workers are more likely to say that extrinsic factors, such as pay and job security, are important. Those in higher-level jobs (which presumably pay better) are more concerned with intrinsic factors, such as the challenge of the job; indeed, they will work for less money if they feel that the job is fulfilling (Powers & Goudy, 1971). These differences by occupational level are probably attributable, again, to differences in expectations. Those in lower-level jobs simply do not expect work to be fulfilling or satisfying. Thus, they are more willing to tolerate boredom for the sake of other, more tangible types of rewards.

Granting these differences in expectations and values, it is still not clear why a given individual regards a particular job as challenging, fulfilling, or satisfying. The explanations offered to answer this question range from the psychoanalytic to the sociological and emphasize a variety of influential factors such as family background, peers, personality characteristics, and availability of options. One concept that may serve to pull together all these threads is that of *congruence.* According to Veroff and Feld (1970):

> To the extent there is congruence between the strength of a motive and the possibilities for the motive to be gratified in the work role, there will be satisfaction and ease in role performance, and to the extent there is poor meshing, there will be problems in the way individuals react to the role [p. 13].

Holland (1973) uses his system of classifying people and occupational environments to operationalize the concept of congruence.

Different types require different environments. For instance, realistic types flourish in realistic environments because such an environment provides the opportunities and rewards a realistic type needs. Incongruence occurs when a type lives in an environment that provides opportunities and rewards foreign to the person's preferences and abilities—for instance, a realistic type in a social environment [pp. 4–5].

Thus, Holland sees congruence and incongruence as the major determinants of job choice, job satisfaction, and job change. By matching the individual's personality with the occupation, one can determine the degree of congruence or incongruence. If a job is congruent with the individual's personality, then presumably he/she will feel satisfied and fulfilled; should that individual be laid off, he/she will look for another job similar in nature. On the other hand, if personality and occupation are incongruent, then presumably the individual will feel frustrated and discontent; if this dissatisfaction is strong enough, and if motivation is high enough, the individual will seek out a new kind of job, even though such a change may entail risk and effort.

How do people happen to find themselves in incongruent jobs? One obvious answer is economic necessity: in times of recession, people may have to take any kind of job they can get. Another answer is that people are forced into making occupational choices before their own interests, values, and abilities are fully clarified. Under pressure from parents, peers, teachers, and counselors, they may make vocational decisions based on inadequate knowledge about themselves and about the world of work; they may drift into the first available job without really considering their options. Not until they have been on the job for a while will they come to feel its incongruence; but at that point, they may be afraid to make a change. And the greater the investment of time, the more unwilling the individual may be to consider changes—or even to admit dissatisfaction

—and the more trapped and helpless he or she may feel.

But perhaps we are placing too much emphasis on negative factors: lack of self-knowledge, lack of information about occupations, external pressures. If one believes that adulthood is a period of change and development, that adults can find new interests or rediscover old interests previously ignored, then it follows that incongruence can result from such changes. A job choice that was initially congruent may become incongruent as the individual develops over time. Studies of career change in adult life (Hiestand, 1971; Schlossberg, 1972) indicate that, while such deep-seated personality changes may not be common, they do occur.

Retirement

A fairly recent phenomenon in human history, retirement from the world of work is generally regarded as a major life transition or turning point —especially for men, whose careers are usually central to their identity. Retirement involves a role deficit—one loses the role of worker—though that loss may be offset by the adoption of new roles, through leisure activity, volunteer work (or even paid second careers), or greater involvement in family life.

Because retirement is generally a predictable and anticipated occurrence and the retired person may have years of life left, it can better be conceived as a long-term process rather than a single event. Seven stages in the process have been identified (Atchley, 1975): (1) *Early preretirement* takes place in middle age, when retirement seems distant. (2) *Near preretirement* is the stage when workers see retirement as imminent and perhaps begin to plan for it; they may gradually withdraw from work activities, taking longer vacations, working only part-time, and so forth. The retirement itself is often marked by a ceremony. (3) In the *honeymoon period,* the newly retired revel in their freedom and perhaps fantasize about what they will do with their time. (4) This may be followed by *disenchantment,* when boredom or depression sets in; often, such negative feelings are triggered by ill health or money problems. (5) A period of *reorientation* is when the retired may seek help in planning for the future. (6) *Stability* is the stage in which the retired make plans and adjustments. (7) *Termination* of the retired role occurs with death, invalidism, or entry into a new career, which may be either a leisure involvement or paid work.

It is often assumed that retirement is traumatic and difficult. Undoubtedly, it does require major adjustment, especially in the individual's allocation of time, and thus may be considered a stress. But the trauma of retirement, like the empty-nest trauma supposedly suffered by women, appears to have been greatly exaggerated. Lowenthal and her associates (1975) found that anxiety about retirement—and especially about possible financial difficulties—was strongest not among the oldest group actually facing retirement but among middle-aged men. The preretirees—especially the men—had generally made their plans and arrangements, felt in control of the situation, and were much more positive in their attitudes. But there are individual differences in reactions to retirement that probably depend upon one's general personality orientation and life circumstances.

Another factor that may influence the individual's attitude is whether the retirement was voluntary or involuntary. One study (Epstein & Murray, 1968) found that only 28% of all workers in 1962 had retired voluntarily; the rest had retired because they were in poor health, had been laid off, or worked for organizations that had a mandatory retirement age. Such people may find retirement a more difficult and troubled time because they have little control over

the decision: it is forced upon them. Those people who must retire earlier than expected—to whom retirement occurs "off time"—may suffer from a sense of worthlessness and age-deviancy and thus may have problems adjusting to being retired.

Nonetheless, many people do make the transition smoothly and without difficulty. To men whose needs for achievement and assertion are being replaced by a need for affiliation, the retirement period may represent an opportunity to fulfill those needs, as well as to pursue other interests that were previously put aside because of job pressures. Women with a primary career commitment may go through much the same reorientation of values as men do, whereas women who have worked without any deep involvement in their jobs may find retirement a welcome time of greater leisure.

Vocational Maturity— A Possibility at Any Age

As was stated previously, most vocational theorists have focused on school-age children and adolescents; the career development of adults had been ignored until recently. At the present time, however, the notion of lifelong vocational development is beginning to make inroads on the concept of stabilization. We have come to recognize that middle age is not necessarily limited to maintaining one's achieved position, nor is it the "beginning of death in life"; for many people, it may be the time for an emerging concept of a lifetime of personal change. Yet we still do not have a firm theoretical base for looking at career development in adults.

Some exceptions include the work of David Sheppard (1971), who has developed an Adult Vocational Maturity Inventory (AVMI) based on Crites's concept of vocational maturity. After administering the AVMI to 200 adult males, Sheppard concluded that "in any large heterogeneous sample of adults, there are individuals who represent all levels of the maturity continuum" (p. 405). Crites is currently developing a model of career development for adulthood (1976).

Vocational maturity is a relevant construct for understanding adult career development in that it encompasses several processes relating to vocational life rather than just the work activity itself. The mature person—whether at age 10, 20, or 50—is the person who is involved in the choice process, is able to make appropriate decisions by first considering expanded alternatives and then narrowing down the options, and is able to utilize existing resources. The point is that the vocationally mature person is open to continuous change—in self and in situation—and is in control of his/her vocational destiny. That such control is rare was dramatically revealed in Anne Roe and Rhoda Baruch's study (1964) of adults who changed careers. Their most striking finding was that these adults did not feel in control of their careers; in fact, they attributed their work changes to chance rather than to deliberate planning.

Vocational maturity may take place at the "normal" point of young adulthood; it may be delayed until later in life; or, conceivably, it may not happen at all for some individuals. Vocational development is not necessarily continuous and sequential; it can be cyclical and may have several stages. For instance, a person may make a rational and mature vocational decision early in life, but then—because of changes in circumstances or in self—the original decision may become inappropriate.

According to Sheppard's (1971) scheme, the more an individual feels self-controlled rather than situation-controlled, the more vocationally mature he/she is. This, then, can be the goal of adult guidance: to intervene in ways that stimulate involvement, orientation, and independence in career decision making. This would result in people's feeling in control of their destinies rather than controlled by external events.

Implications for Counseling

The following points summarize the discussion as it applies to the counselor's task of trying to help clients take control of their vocational lives.

1. Virtually every individual's work history is characterized by change of some sort, slight or drastic, voluntary or involuntary. A person may change employers but remain in essentially the same field at the same level; may move up the status hierarchy; may make minor or major changes in field; may retire from paid employment completely. Such changes usually involve a reassessment of self and adjustment to the new situation. Indeed, even workers who stay in the same job at the same level through their entire working lives may be said to experience change relative to others and to their own expectations. The nonoccurrence of an anticipated event (such as a job promotion) also requires stock-taking and adjustment.

2. The most useful construct for understanding career development and job satisfaction is *congruence:* how the person's needs, interests, and preferences "fit" with the opportunities and rewards offered by the work environment. If the individual and the occupation are congruent, the result will probably be job satisfaction; if incongruent, dissatisfaction will result. Lack of self-awareness and of knowledgeability about the world of work may lead people to make incongruent choices. In addition, an initially congruent choice can become incongruent if the person's interests, values, and needs change. The concept of congruence can serve as a guide for intervention. As adults discuss their problems with the counselor, both can work on pinpointing the causes and extent of dissonance between personality and job. This clarification is a first step in exploring new career options, formulat-

ing new goals, and seeking ways to implement these goals.

3. Just as work is of central importance in the lives of most Americans, so the concept of control is of central importance in understanding vocational development—including the retirement process—in adults. People who feel in control, who believe that their decisions and actions will make a difference, will be able to make more appropriate choices. In contrast, those who feel that the locus of control lies outside themselves will be too apathetic even to attempt to exercise choice. It is the responsibility of the counselor to help clients regain a sense of control by pointing out to them expanded alternatives, by offering them guidance in narrowing down options, and by making them aware of existing resources.

INTERPERSONAL RELATIONS

Human beings are social animals and, in the course of their lives, form various kinds of dyadic relationships with other human beings. Lowenthal and her associates (1975) differentiate four basic types of dyadic relationship: (1) acquaintanceship, (2) friendly interaction, (3) friendship, and (4) intimacy. These form a continuum based on an increase in knowledge of the uniqueness of the other individuals and in involvement with them and a decrease in stereotyped, formal, and role-reliant activities and behavior toward them. To put it another way, we tend to identify strangers (especially those with whom we expect to have no further interaction) by the roles they play: the bus driver, the usher, the store clerk. Acquaintances are those people with whom we have some recurring interaction but whom we still probably perceive primarily in their roles and treat with some formality. At each further step along the continuum, we are less conscious of the role and more conscious of the indi-

vidual personality; formality decreases and spontaneity grows.

Erikson (1950) regards intimacy as the first major developmental crisis of adulthood, following the formation of ego identity in adolescence. Gruen (1964), working with Erikson's theoretical model, defines intimacy as "mutuality with a loved partner of the opposite sex with whom one is able to regulate the cycles of work, procreation, and recreation" (p. 2). Failure to resolve that crisis, he believes, results in isolation and disturbs further development. Though Erikson's theory is difficult to test empirically, the San Francisco study of adults at four pretransitional stages (Lowenthal et al., 1975) tends to confirm the general notion that close interpersonal relations are important to adjustment and suggests that the need for intimacy continues throughout the life course.

Defining interpersonal intimacy as a relationship characterized by similarity, reciprocity, and compatibility, Lowenthal and Weiss (1976) maintain that "close interpersonal relationships serve as a resource against life's crises" (p. 14). They suggest, however, that the correlation between adjustment and intimacy varies by sex and by stage. In general, the need for affiliation is stronger in women, who tend to form more complex interpersonal relations than do men. In American society particularly, men are expected to suppress their affiliative needs, whereas women are freer to express affection and to show emotion. As suggested in Chapter 2, assertiveness and achievement are taken to be the bailiwick of the male, and affiliation and nurturance the bailiwick of the female—though there seems to be a crossover in these sex roles at some point in the middle years. The failure of each sex to allow fuller development to both sides of the personality early in life may result in frustration and despair later on, when the suppressed side asserts itself. At that point, women may find it impossible to break out of the domestic bind in which they have tied themselves, and men may find it impossible to build up relationships which they have earlier slighted or ignored.

In addition, Lowenthal and Weiss found that the need for intimate relations as a buffer against stress varies over time. Thus, the relation between intimacy and adjustment as measured by satisfaction and by absence of psychological and physical symptoms of disorder was weakest among the group who were high school seniors at the time of the initial interviews; stronger among newlywed women, but not newlywed men, at the time of the initial interview, but not at the two followup points (18 months later and 5 years later), when most had had children; and even stronger among both middle-aged and preretirement men and women 18 months after the initial survey, but not 5 years later.

Not all interpersonal relationships are characterized by intimacy and mutuality, of course. In this section, we will be considering a broad range of relationships: friendship, relations with family of origin (one's parents, siblings, and other kin), the marital relationship, and parenthood.

Friendship

The term *friendship* is somewhat elastic, implying different degrees of closeness and intimacy to different people. The notion of a "best friend" or a "close friend" connotes mutual supportiveness, trust, the exchange of confidences, and in the early stages, frequent interaction. Once intimacy is established, however, proximity seems to make little difference, and people will continue to consider themselves close friends though they have had no direct contact for a number of years. Making friends seems to be connected with developing a sense of identity; and it may be that people with whom we have made friends during early adulthood serve as a

reference point in our lives and give us a sense of continuity with our own past.

Consistent with the sex differences reported earlier, women tend to have more friends (by their own reports), to be more deeply involved with them, and to have more complex perceptions of them (as reflected in the degree of detail with which they described them) than do men (Weiss & Lowenthal, 1975). In addition, they are more likely to make confidantes of their friends and to emphasize reciprocity and good communication as essential in friendship. Men, on the other hand, are more likely to stress similarity—common experiences and activities, similar interests and behavior—as the basis of friendship; they look less for understanding and acceptance and are more likely to say that their wives are their confidantes.

In describing the qualities of real and ideal friendships, however, both sexes in the San Francisco study were likely to mention similarity in talking about their real friends but qualities related to reciprocity (supportiveness, understanding, acceptance, trust) in talking about ideal friendships. The implication is that people would prefer to have as friends people who will listen to their confidences and give them support in a nonjudgmental way, but in actuality tend to have as friends people with whom they have shared experiences and activities. Compatibility—simple enjoyment of being with the other person—was also mentioned fairly frequently as a quality of friendship, both real and ideal (Weiss & Lowenthal, 1975).

Adults usually select friends from among people at the same point in development; indeed, stage is generally more important than chronological age. A 40-year-old couple will find a 20-year-old couple compatible if both have children the same age. Moreover, the nature of the friendship varies through the life course.

Young couples usually have two sets of

friends: individuals of the same sex and similar interests, in many cases old friends from the days before marriage; and "family friends," other couples whom they may see regularly and with whom they form ties on the basis of their work or interests. Middle-class young couples are more likely to have "family friends," whereas among working-class couples, friendships tend to be sex-segregated and to be formed with relatives or neighbors rather than with work associates. Young couples report having the greatest number of friends and interacting with them more frequently. Young adults are also much more likely than older adults to mention cross-sex friends, though this difference may represent a generational effect rather than a function of increasing age. Because of the incipient sexuality of a man/ woman relationship, cross-sex friendships are rare.

The middle-aged couples in the San Francisco study had fewer friends than the other age groups, were less likely to share "family friends," engaged in less social interaction, and were more simplistic in describing their friends. It may be that at this stage of life, workers are too involved with their jobs and homemakers too involved with their families to spend much time and energy on extrafamilial interpersonal relations. Moreover, adults in this age group are more likely than are younger adults to be involved in formal organizations—political, cultural, professional—and thus to have a network of acquaintances. Finally, it is possible that at this stage of life, adults still feel the closest ties with friends whom they made in earlier years, who now may be geographically distant.

Among preretirement adults, however, the need for close personal interactions outside the family seems to reassert itself. Weiss and Lowenthal (1975) report that next to the newlyweds, people in the preretirement stage had the largest number of friends, and that their perceptions of their friends were more complex than at any other stage. Inter-

estingly, the discrepancy between real and ideal friends was greatest at this stage, perhaps because older people idealize old friends whom they have lost through death or distance, but more likely because at this point, freed from career and family pressures, people "become more concerned with interpersonal relationships and more interested in the complexities of human nature. Such an increase in perceptual and conceptual sensitivity would, of course, allow for a greater discrepancy between the real and the ideal" (Weiss & Lowenthal, 1975, pp. 58–59).

The importance of friendship among older people is reflected in the finding (Lowenthal & Haven, 1968) that those who maintain at least one intimate relationship can survive other losses and remain functioning in society, whereas those who cannot claim intimacy with another human being are more likely to suffer psychological and even physical disabilities and to become institutionalized.

Relations with Family and Kin

We hear a great deal these days—usually accompanied by weeping, wailing, and wringing of hands—about the plight of the isolated nuclear family (husband, wife, and dependent children) and the dire social consequences that flow from the disintegration of the extended-family system, in which a host of relatives, near and distant, were always ready to step in to help other family members when needed, to provide the individual with a sense of cohesiveness and of integration into the larger society, and to provide the young with suitable role models. According to this view, because industrialization and urbanization demand mobility on the part of workers, young adults have moved out of the rural areas and into the cities, becoming separated from their parents and other relatives. In a country as large as the United States, such movement may involve enormous distances. Thus, the argument runs, the nuclear family exists virtually on its own, rootless and vulnerable.

But the death of the extended-family system has been greatly exaggerated. There is ample evidence to show that the "modified extended family," comprising "nuclear families bound together by affectional ties and by choice" (Sussman & Burchinal, 1962) is the system that now operates. Adults maintain contact with their parents, though they rarely live together under the same roof except in cases of extreme poverty or physical incapacity. Indeed, studies have found that about three in five people over age 65 live within walking distance of at least one of their children, and that a larger proportion live in the same community. Adults who are single, widowed, or divorced are more likely to live close to their parents than those who are married, and younger adults are more likely to live near their parents than are middle-aged adults. Interaction is frequent, if not by visitation then by telephone calls; and mutual aid is exchanged, in the form of money, gifts, or services such as child care, help with housework, and care during sickness. Most such aid flows from parents to children, although middle-aged adults may have to aid both their adult children and their aging parents.

Rarely do adults reject their parents. They continue to feel close to them and, out of a sense of obligation, may even "take care of their aged and ill parents themselves when they should instead be arranging for them to get medical care and treatment" (Troll, 1975, p. 104),* failing to recognize that many of the disabilities of age are not inevitable but can be treated. Though feelings of love and

*From *Early and Middle Adulthood: The Best Is Yet to Be—Maybe*, by L. E. Troll. Copyright © 1975 by Wadsworth Publishing Company, Inc. This and all other quotations from this source are reprinted by permission of the publisher, Brooks/Cole Publishing Company, Monterey, California.

affection toward parents are not necessarily related to degree of interaction or extent of aid given, most adults do show strong affection for their parents. For instance, young married couples spend a considerable amount of time talking to each other about their parents (Feldman, 1964). Even after they have died, parents may continue to occupy the thoughts of their middle-aged children, who perhaps for the first time are coming to see their parents as real people—thus reaching the point of *filial maturity* (Blenkner, 1965).

Because of such long-range demographic trends as increased life span, earlier marriage and childbearing, and the consequent shortening of the time span between generations, four-generation families have become fairly common. In 1962, close to one in four people age 65 and over in the United States reported that they were great-grandparents (Townsend, 1968). Family relationships and behavior patterns have changed somewhat, becoming more complex. For instance, because grandparents now tend to be younger than they were 50 years ago and thus to have a surviving spouse, to be busy with their own homes and careers, and to be socially active, they are probably less deeply involved with their grandchildren and more apt to play the role of "fun seeker" (Neugarten & Weinstein, 1964) than of authority figures.

Adults are generally not so close to their siblings or to more distant kin as to their parents, although the extended family may draw together again in times of stress or on ritual occasions, such as weddings and funerals. The extent of interaction varies by socioeconomic status, with working-class families usually more close-knit than middle- and upper-class families. Lower-class family members are likely not only to live in closer geographic proximity, but also to give aid in the form of direct services; more affluent families tend to give aid in the form of money and gifts, so that the young couple can live up to an approved standard. Lower-class women frequently select their close friends from among their relatives (such as sisters or female cousins). Certain ethnic groups, too, may give greater emphasis to the extended family and engage more frequently in such ceremonial activities as family reunions.

Again, sex differences with respect to family relations are pronounced. It is usually the wife who takes responsibility for maintaining contact with her own and her husband's family. If the couple is divorced, or if the wife dies, the husband's ties with his own family may be weakened, and his contact with in-laws usually ends entirely. Conversely, parents tend to remain closer to their daughters than to their sons, though if the daughter marries "beneath" her, this relation may be strained.

The effective functioning of the modified extended family is attributable to further technological advances in industrial society, which was previously blamed for the destruction of the extended family. Improved systems of communication and transportation have made frequent interaction among nuclear families possible, even when they live some distance from one another. Undoubtedly, with the modification of the extended family, certain other features of family life have changed considerably: the structure is no longer hierarchical and authoritarian, and decision making is left to the nuclear family unit.

The Marital Relationship

Over the last 100 years or so, gradual demographic shifts have changed the shape, so to speak, of married life. First, life expectancy has lengthened by several decades. Second, couples have tended to marry younger, to have their first child sooner, and to have fewer children but with shorter intervals between births. Though people reach social maturity somewhat earlier, economic maturity is often delayed, as more young men and women continue on to college and remain to some extent dependent on their parents and other family members for financial support. Another common pattern is for the wife to work to help pay for the husband's graduate or professional education. Because of general affluence, however, young people today start married life relatively well-off in terms of durable goods and financial security. In 1890, a marriage was usually terminated by the death of husband or wife about 2 years before the youngest child had departed from the parental home; today, the last child leaves the nest while the parents are still relatively young. Thus, a postparental period, which lasts perhaps 20 years and during which husband and wife are again alone together, has come into being.

Further shifts may now be in progress that could drastically affect the marital relationship. For instance, there seems to be a growing tendency to delay marriage, perhaps attributable to the tighter economy of the 1970s, perhaps to a growing valuation of personal freedom and a desire for self-expression, particularly among women. Birth rates continue to decline, especially among the educated middle class. Couples are delaying having children, and some are deciding not to have children at all. But these tendencies have not yet become sufficiently pronounced, or continued long enough, to be called trends. Marriage with children still remains both the ideal and the norm. Moreover, even though divorce rates are up, most divorced persons remarry. If marriage is a convenience for men, it is an absolute necessity for women in the eyes of society: the terms *spinster* and *old maid* remain pejorative in a way that the term *bachelor* never was.

Nonetheless, contrary to popular belief, the married state seems to be more beneficial to men than to women, at least in terms of mental health.

Wives are likely to be more conscious of and more troubled by marital problems than are men, whose identity is usually tied to their jobs. Lowenthal and her associates (1975) found that the middle-aged women in their middle-class, highly family-centered sample were especially apt to be unhappy, often bitter about their lost chances, and to show signs of maladjustment. Bernard (1972) cites copious evidence to show that married men and single women are better adjusted than single men and married women. Single men were the most psychologically impaired group; they were passive, antisocial, and highly subject to depression. But married women were much more likely than were either single women or married men to suffer from depression, passivity, and phobic tendencies, and to report symptoms of psychological distress. Apparently, women invest more in marriage, are socialized to suppress their own individuality and desires, and may end up paying a heavier cost.

In American society, people marry for love and companionship. Like tends to pair off with like, in terms of social class, family background, and values. If anything, it is the woman who is expected to "marry up": the woman who marries a man younger than herself, or one perceptibly less educated and intelligent, or of substantially lower social class, is thought to have made a "bad marriage" and is regarded as deviant. On the average, men marry at age 23 and women at age 20, both sexes having been socialized to heterosexual attitudes and relationships by dating—at various levels of intensity—through high school and college. The wedding itself is still treated as a special occasion, with four in five couples having a religious ceremony.

The roles of husband and wife are clearly differentiated in the traditional marriage. The husband is expected to be the breadwinner and the buffer between the family and the outside world. The wife is given primary responsibility for keeping house and raising the children; at the same time, she is expected to be companion and partner to the husband. In the early years of marriage, when the children are young, the husband is likely to be more involved in helping the wife with household tasks and in spending time with the children, but over the years, the husband's interest in these activities usually wanes. In addition to her primary tasks, the wife may go to work, particularly after her children are in school, to help supplement the family income, but she is not expected to devote time and energy to a career. Sometimes she participates in child-centered activities, such as PTA and Scouts. If the husband holds a relatively high-status position, the wife may also be expected to entertain business associates in order to further her husband's career. Though housekeeping tasks are not intrinsically satisfying to many people, many women may find expression for their achievement drive by such means as keeping an immaculate house, doing their own decorating, or engaging in other more innovative but still female-typed activities such as baking their own bread, hooking rugs, and so forth.

Role differentiation in marriage is probably most pronounced among the less educated, the working class, and older people. It is often associated with the proximity of an extended family, which enables the wife to rely on her female relatives rather than her husband for companionship and help. There is likely to be more sharing of tasks and less role differentiation among the educated middle class and among younger people. Indeed, the college-educated man is likely to experience role conflicts because he is expected to be more involved with his family, sharing leisure activities with wife and children, at the time when he also should be devoting energy to getting ahead in his career. Though the popular media emphasize a trend away from the traditional marriage and toward a more egalitarian arrangement, it is still too early to tell how widespread or long-lasting such a shift may be. As Troll (1975) puts it:

> Just as we have had to modify our predictions about the demise of the extended family, we must modify our predictions about the demise of traditional marital-role differentiation. Present-day husbands and wives are probably neither so differentiated in function or behavior as some family theorists believe nor so interchangeable as others assert. Furthermore, perceptions of role changes may be greater than the actual changes. . . . More change has probably taken place in ideology than in behavior. . . . On the other hand, ideology may really be the forerunner of new behavior [pp. 84–85].

Various kinds of relatively predictable developmental patterns occur in the marital relationship and in family life generally. For instance, Hill, Foote, Aldous, Carlson, and Macdonald (1968) found that the volume of financial activity is highest in the early years of marriage (when the young couple is acquiring a home and durable goods and having children), then levels off and slowly declines over the remaining years; residential moves, occupational changes, and complexity of family interactions all follow the same pattern. The husband's authority as a decision maker is also strongest in the early years, until the children are in school, and then it, too, slowly declines—perhaps because there are fewer major decisions to be made (Hill et al., 1968).

Another pattern common enough to seem almost inevitable is the gradual decrease in intimacy between husband and wife, as manifested by fewer demonstrations of affection, sexual boredom, a drop in sexual activity between the marriage partners (with some husbands and wives having extramarital affairs), a decrease in companionship, and a loss of common interests. This process has been labeled *disenchantment* (Pineo, 1961). It generally occurs over a 20-year period, though the process is speeded up among couples who were married in high school, with disenchantment occurring after only 18 months of marriage. The loss of intimacy is often blamed on the presence of children (adolescent children seem to put an especially great strain on the marital relationship), but childless couples, too, seem to grow apart.

The disenchantment process was reflected, in the San Francisco study, in how people at various stages described their spouses (Thurnher, 1975). Newlyweds were most apt to mention personality characteristics and emotional responsiveness, whereas the two older groups (middle-aged parents and preretirees) were more likely to describe their spouses in terms of normative role expectations— the husband as a "good provider," the wife as a "good mother" or "efficient housekeeper." At all three stages, married couples were generally positive in their descriptions; the exception was the middle-aged women, who were the most likely of any group to use negative or ambivalent terms in describing their husbands. Kerckhoff and Bean (1970) suggest that there is an inverse relation between role structure and the interpersonal components of a dyadic relationship: that is, when two people are closely involved with one another, responding to each other's unique characteristics, they are less likely to think in terms of normative roles.

The explanation for disenchantment as an almost inevitable process lies in the selective nature of the marital relation. People do not marry at random; they select partners whose backgrounds, interests, and values are congruent with their own. But the individuals making up the couple change and develop over time, and the odds are against their developing in the same direction. Table 3-1 illustrates the various possibilities for development in the relationship as the husband and the wife

TABLE 3-1. Potential development of the husband-wife relationship

Development of Husband	Development of Wife		
	None (stable)	Becomes more complex	Becomes less complex
None (stable)	Match should remain good. Perhaps dormant while children intervene, but, when they leave, may get "second honeymoon."	Match deteriorates. Wife's needs no longer met.	Match deteriorates. Husband's needs no longer met.
Becomes more complex	Match deteriorates. Husband's needs no longer met.	Relationship has chance to develop if individuals' changes are on same path. But they could each develop in different directions and would no longer match.	Match deteriorates. Husband's needs no longer met.
Becomes less complex	Match deteriorates. Wife's needs no longer met.	Match deteriorates. Wife's needs no longer met.	Relationship has chance of staying matched if negative developments of both are synchronous; could be like "cooling off." But if not, synchronization will disappear.

From *Early and Middle Adulthood: The Best Is Yet to Be—Maybe,* by L. E. Troll. Copyright © 1975 by Wadsworth Publishing Company, Inc. Reprinted by permission of the publisher, Brooks/Cole Publishing Company, Monterey, California.

become more complex, less complex, or remain pretty much the same. As is obvious, the chances for a match remaining congruent are small, but they do exist. If both partners remain stable, undergoing no drastic changes in personality; or if both develop toward greater complexity, and in the same way (for example, developing the same new interests); or if both move toward less complexity, and in the same way, then the fit may remain close.

The marital relationship can also be analyzed as a system (see Chapter 2) that reacts to change (for instance, the birth of a child, or a major career change by one of the partners) by compensating for it in order to maintain equilibrium, by incorporating it to produce development of the system, either positive or negative, or by breaking down.

It should be noted that disenchantment is not synonymous with dissatisfaction or unhappiness. The individual's reaction to loss of intimacy with the mate seems to depend on his or her expectations. More highly educated people, who place a higher value on companionship and reciprocity, are more likely to be unhappy when the marriage relationship cools off; whereas those with a more traditional view of marriage, who place a higher value on instrumental roles, may not be troubled by the decrease in intimacy.

Special mention should be made of the postparental period in the marriage relation. Historically speaking, it is a relatively new period, and there are two opposed views about it. The first view is that it places a severe strain on the marital relation; with the children gone, husbands and wives no longer have any common interest. The second view is that it represents a "second honeymoon," when husbands and wives rediscover each other, free from the distraction of children.

Irwin Deutscher (1964), surveying upper-middle-class and lower-middle-class families in Kansas City, found that most couples in the postparental stage evaluated it favorably. Of those who had a negative view, most attributed their dissatisfaction to physical disabilities (such as the menopause), to a sense of personal failure (such as not being a good parent), or to feelings of emptiness and an inability to fill the gap. Women were more inclined than men to have strong reactions, whether favorable or unfavorable. The middle-aged parents among the San Francisco subjects (Thurnher, 1975) also looked forward to the empty nest as a time of greater companionship with their mates; the preretirees, who were in the postparental period, reported that their marriage had improved when the children were gone, though this response was more common among men than women. Men at this point apparently expect increased attention from their wives: it is significant that older women were more likely than all other groups except newly-wed men to report that their spouses were too dependent on them.

Thus the postparental period is not without its problems, particularly in view of the crossover in sex roles that may occur. Women may want to use their new freedom to pursue interests in the external world just at the point when their husbands are interested in fulfilling their needs for affiliation and look forward to being coddled by their wives.

Despite longer life expectancy and the prospect of some years together after the children leave home, one of the partners—usually the husband—is still likely to die earlier than the other. What is generally not recognized is that half of all widows in the United States (not counting those who have remarried) are under age 60 (Lopata, 1973). The younger widow is in many ways worse off than the older widow, who has generally "rehearsed" for widowhood and who, moreover, has other friends in the same position. But the death of a spouse is a traumatic event for both sexes, ranking at the top of the Holmes/Rahe Social Readjustment Scale (1967; see Chapters 2 and 7.) Indeed, the life expectancy of the surviving spouse is shortened by 5 years following bereavement (Parkes, 1964). Men may find the death of a spouse more traumatic than women do, partly because they are less prepared for it and partly because they have no other person with whom they are intimate (Lowenthal & Weiss, 1976).

Many marriages terminate before the death of one of the partners, of course. In 1965, about three in ten marriages ended in divorce; in 1971, the figures had risen to two in five (Weiss, 1975). Not only are divorce rates increasing, but they are rising at all age levels, though they are still highest in the early years of a marriage. The factors that make one couple stay married and another couple get divorced are complex. Dissatisfaction and unhappiness are not sufficient causes. Socioeconomic status, religion, values, and the expectations of the individuals involved may all play a part in the decision to divorce or to remain married. Longer life expectancy may also be a significant factor, in that people are less willing to face the prospect of 40 more years (rather than 10 more years) of unhappy marriage.

Whatever the factors involved in divorce, both partners are subject to severe stress and trauma. The woman is probably more vulnerable than the man, however, especially if she is traditional in her views and has defined her own identity through her husband. Since marriage and family are viewed as the woman's domain, the failure of a marriage seems to reflect a failure on the part of the wife. If she is given custody of the children, not only may she bear severe financial strains, but also she may find it difficult to start dating again. Since she automatically loses the "family friends" that she shared with her husband, she is likely to be cast adrift socially.

Nonetheless, divorced women under the age of 30 are the most likely of any group—men or women, single, divorced, or widowed—to marry. The second most likely to marry are divorced men. There are racial differences in both divorce and remarriage rates, with Black men and women having higher divorce rates and lower remarriage rates than White men and women. But most divorced people do remarry. In 1971, over 10% of the men and over 14% of the women in the United States had been married at least twice (Troll, 1975).

The appropriateness of the traditional monogamous marriage has been called into question in recent years, and new forms of marriage have been proposed. The social and historical changes behind such thinking include longer life expectancy, which may make a lifetime commitment to another person less realistic, or at least less acceptable; an emphasis on having fewer—or even no—children, as the over-population problem becomes more visible; reduction in infant mortality rates, which means that children are more likely to reach maturity and thus that a large number of births is not necessary to ensure family continuity; technological developments that render physical strength a less meaningful job requirement, giving women a better chance in the job market and freeing them from economic dependence on men; the supplementation and sub-

stitution of home services, so that a man no longer requires a full-time housekeeper; less intimacy and greater superficiality in other human relations as a result of increased mobility; and a general spirit of exploring new lifestyles and rejecting the old and the traditional. The new forms proposed range all the way from "swinging" through intimate networks to group marriages. So far, none of these forms is practiced by any but a very small proportion of people. The ideal of marriage for life is still dominant.

Parenthood

The sharply differing roles that men and women in our society play in raising their children is nowhere better reflected than in the fact that, as commonly used, the verb *to mother* means to care for tenderly, to nurture, whereas the verb *to father* means simply to beget. Of course, in actuality, the father's part goes far beyond the biological act of procreation. Nonetheless, just as the woman generally has primary responsibility for housekeeping, so she has primary responsibility for child care. When one reflects that the average age of the woman at marriage is 20, that two-thirds of White mothers and three-fourths of non-White mothers have their first baby by the end of the second year of marriage, and that young women in our society have virtually no preparental preparation or training in caring for infants, it should come as no surprise that many young women find motherhood extremely distressing.

According to LeMasters (1957), the entire period before and after the birth of the first child constitutes a crisis in mental health. Not only is the young mother often physically exhausted, anxious about her ability to carry out her new maternal duties, resentful over having to curtail all her other activities, and possibly angry at her husband because his freedom seems to continue undiminished, but she may also suffer from guilt at having such negative feelings—especially when she has been socialized to believe that bearing and caring for babies is the greatest joy in a woman's life. Older women, women who delay having children until later in marriage, and women who have "lived" a little in the outside world may be better able to handle the sudden demands of being a new mother, although LeMasters suggests that women who have previously had careers are under a double stress: they have had to give up the career, and they have had to assume the responsibilities of motherhood.

Just as the infant is affected by the kind of mothering it receives, so the mother is affected by the infant's behavior. Some mothers and infants seem to be better matched than others. Moreover, sex and birth order influence maternal behavior. Thus, mothers seem to exert greater control—and for a longer period of time—over their daughters, but they may give more praise to their sons. They are also likely to be more involved with, and more anxious about, the firstborn than later children—though this does not imply that they love the later-born children less. Fashions in child rearing fluctuate from one generation to the next, and vary by social class, from strict to permissive. The degree of control or permissiveness with which the mother treats the child bears no relation to the love or hostility she feels toward that child.

Being a mother is something of a no-win situation. A woman's lack of training in child-rearing practices—indeed, the lack of agreement in our society about what constitute appropriate child-rearing practices—coupled with her almost total responsibility and with the conviction that the competent mother can raise superior children, makes it almost impossible for her to feel that she has been successful. The working-class or less educated woman is more likely to feel resentful toward her children because they were unplanned, because there are too many of them, and because often she must raise them without a husband; in any case, she is likely to end up feeling guilty over her resentment and hostility. The middle-class or better-educated woman may not have the same disadvantages to cope with but is likely to have unrealistic expectations and standards, so that she too is likely to end up feeling guilty (Lopata, 1971).

The attitudes and behavior of the father depend to a considerable extent on his social class, educational level, and age. Thus, the working-class and less-educated father is more distant from his children, less involved in their care, and more authoritarian in his treatment of them. In addition, he may become more uncomfortable with them as he anticipates the day when they will surpass him in education and come to recognize his low status (Veroff & Feld, 1970). The young father, who is likely not to have achieved financial independence, is also likely to be uninvolved with his children, resentful of them, and even neglectful or harsh in his treatment of them. Men who become fathers at age 33 or older seem to be much more comfortable in their roles, more concerned with their children, more objective, and more aware of their responsibility as role models (Nydegger, 1973). Generally, fathers are more involved with their children during the first 2 months of infancy but then tend to withdraw, though it is not clear whether they do so out of choice, out of a need to devote their energies to the breadwinner role, or because that is the way their wives want it.

The age of the children affects the relationship between the parents. The intimate bond between husband and wife may be strengthened when the children are infants or very young, but having adolescents around the house seems to impose strains on everyone involved and to have an unfavorable effect on the marital relationship. Husbands are less affected than wives by the approach of the empty nest, but both partners may benefit when the children actually depart from home, and a second honeymoon may ensue. Paul Bohannon (1971) has remarked that "middle-class Americans establish a sort of antithesis between parenting and spousing," and that parenting seems to "interfere with the capacities of a spouse either to give or to receive attention and love from the other spouse" (p. 58). The San Francisco study (Lowenthal et al., 1975) seems to confirm this observation.

Although a trend toward the father's taking on a greater share of child-rearing responsibilities may be in the making, it is too early to say whether a lessening of sex-role differentiation in parenting is mostly a matter of talk or is a behavioral fact. Certainly, the difficulty of the mother's role seems to be more widely recognized, and various kinds of arrangements to relieve her of some of the burden—such as cooperative households, child-care facilities, foster grandparents—are being tried out. Another, and perhaps more clearly defined, trend is for parents to have fewer children. It may also be that more young couples are deciding to remain childless. Children do not necessarily make a marriage, as is commonly believed; indeed, childless couples tend to report happier marriages than couples who have children (Blood & Wolfe, 1960;

Feldman, 1964). Nonetheless, most people still marry with the expectation of having children.

Implications for Counseling

The following points summarize the discussion as it applies to the counselor's role.

1. Counselors must look beyond the fact of marriage and parenthood to see if the client has achieved, or is capable of achieving, intimacy. The finding that intimacy is an effective buffer against stress reemphasizes that it is the process of intimacy, and not the fact of marriage or parenthood, that is the key to coping with life's stresses. Although the family is here to stay, many married partners become disenchanted and lose the closeness so essential to a feeling of hope and well-being.

2. Although most people still opt for traditional patterns in their interpersonal relations, many do not. The counselor needs to confront his/her own values about what is a workable lifestyle in order not to influence clients who hold different values. Good adjustment is possible in a variety of personal relations and lifestyles.

3. The arenas of work and interpersonal relations shift in saliency throughout the life span. Adults can "recycle" several times during their lives and often need help in making such transitions.

For activities and skills related to this chapter, see Chapter 8.

4

Interventions: Focus on Counseling

Traditionally, the chief type of intervention practiced by the counselor has been the counseling activity itself: working in a face-to-face situation either with the individual client or with groups of clients, listening and responding to their problems, helping them to understand those problems and to make adaptive decisions. (A second type of intervention, program development, is covered in Chapter 5; a third type, social action, is touched on in "A Final Word.")

It is the belief of the authors that counseling adults requires special knowledge and skills. To an extent not true of children and adolescents, adults have an identity, a history, a long-range perspective on time. During their lives, they have probably passed through various transitions and role changes, learned certain coping skills, experienced and observed much of life. Their greater experience, longer time perspective, and broader view of their history can be used as resources, so that client and counselor together can build a foundation for dealing with particular problems and can develop strategies for handling future problems.

The danger of responding to adults as though they were teenagers was dramatically illustrated a few years ago at a workshop for counselors of adults, where a panel of middle-aged men, all of whom had recently returned to college, were invited to talk about their past histories, their goals, and their experiences in coming back to school. One recurrent motif was indignation toward the counselors and academic advisors they had encountered in college. These men had demonstrated their competence and their high motivation. One was a policeman who had risen to the top ranks of his force, another was a factory worker who had become a foreman, a third was a school janitor so devoted to the ideals of education that he had put his daughters through college. All had, in one way or another, proved themselves in the nonacademic world. Yet because many of them had poor or erratic high school records and borderline test scores, the counselors questioned their eligibility for admission to college—thus ignoring 20 or more years of steady achievement. The counselor of adults must be able to look beyond chronological age, test scores, and high school grades in dealing with clients.

Moreover, in the opinion of the authors, the counselor who takes a static view of adulthood (see Chapter 2), trying to force the client to behave according to some preconceived standard of "maturity," or to "adjust" to some socially accepted but personally unfulfilling situation, is doing a disservice to the client. Such an authoritarian approach may work in the short run but is ineffective over the long run, ignoring as it does the client's need to develop an internal locus of control. The counselor should regard the adult client as a partner in the working out of solutions; the effort should be a joint one.

This chapter first presents two sample interviews, with comments, to illustrate a workable approach to several issues in adulthood. It then discusses some of the special components of counseling adults.

TWO SAMPLE INTERVIEWS

When the client enters the room, the counselor is able to observe that he is a man about 45 years old who seems to be particularly nervous. He sits on the edge of the chair opposite the counselor and immediately begins to twirl the wedding band on his finger.

Interview	Comments
Counselor: We have about an hour together today. Maybe we can begin by discussing what we want to do during that time.	*Counselor begins by structuring the session.*
Client: Well, I'm not sure exactly why I'm here today. It's just that a number of things have happened to me lately that make me feel as though my whole world is coming apart.	
Counselor: You're feeling as if you've been bombarded with a number of things recently.	*The counselor tries to help identify with the client's feelings of despair and to begin clarifying the issues.*
Client: Yes, I feel as if I'm not quite the same person I was a year ago.	
Counselor: I hear almost a sense of heaviness and despair in your voice.	*Again, an attempt to focus on the feelings the client is expressing in order to build rapport.*
Client: Yes, it's my job and my marriage. I don't know what happened, but they both seemed to go sour at the same time. I used to be excited about the work I did. I'm a plasma physicist and used to be very involved in my research. I work in an R & D organization that's always on the cutting edge of technology. But that's no longer exciting to me.	
Counselor: Work no longer offers the same kind of challenge.	*Counselor attempts to focus on work rather than marriage for the moment.*
Client: I'm not even sure I'm in the right field anymore. I went into this field because I liked doing research and being involved in fairly creative, intellectual activities. I also liked working with people—and at the time a merging of the two interests didn't seem that impossible. But what's happened lately is that I'm pretty much involved in solitary work—in my lab by myself. I miss the interaction with people.	

Counselor: Any opportunity to interact with people in a meaningful way is missing.

Client: That's right. Sometimes I find myself talking out loud—carrying on a conversation with myself. Something happened about three weeks ago, though, that I want to talk to you about. I went to this training course on T.A. and for the first time in a long time I felt myself getting elated. I was with people and I was learning about a way to deal with people.

Counselor: As you're telling me about the course now, I can hear your enthusiasm.

Client: What happened afterward though was that I was getting all these crazy thoughts—I kinda scared myself —maybe I should throw it all in and try to get into a field where I can have more contact with people. Boy, all these crazy thoughts raced through my head. I was almost ready to write a letter of resignation.

Counselor: It sounds as though your feelings of impetuousness were a little scary.

Client: Yes, I was scared, but on the other hand I know if I don't kick myself in the ass and do something quickly I'm going to spend whatever short time I have left by myself in my lab.

Counselor: You seem to be feeling a sense of time urgency: if I don't do it now, I may never do it.

Client: Well, you know what it's like. You have all these hot-shot dreams about putting the world on fire when you begin working, and then 20 years later you find yourself like me. And the hardest part is—I'll probably go on bitching and moaning until somebody forces me to change.

Counselor: You feel as though you didn't quite meet the dreams of your youth, and you're angry at yourself for not doing anything about it before time runs out.

Client: Yes, I'm sure I want to change what I want to be doing in my work, but I'm not sure where to start and I'm not sure I'll go through with it.

Counselor: Well, that sounds like one area we can work on together: we can begin to identify possible new areas of work and how you can move into those areas. How does that sound?

Client: That sounds pretty good. I think I'd be better off thinking through any move I was going to make rather than just acting on one of those crazy ideas I had.

Counselor: When we began today, you said that both your job and your marriage had gone sour. Is your marriage something you'd like to talk more about?

Client: Yes, I guess so—I guess like my job I'm beginning

Counselor tries to clarify the feelings and issues of "non-fit" related to work.

Counselor responds to the change in voice inflection and tone.

Counselor responds to feelings expressed.

Counselor begins to introduce information on time perspective.

Counselor tries to introduce the notion of a gap between the dream and present reality.

Counselor begins to introduce a decision-making strategy.

Counselor picks up on an issue that was introduced earlier by client.

to wonder if I should stick with my marriage. There just doesn't seem to be any point in it anymore.

Counselor: You're beginning to ask whether there's anything left to be saved.

Client: Yes, we just don't talk to one another anymore. The romance was worn out a long time ago.

Counselor: What was a meaningful relationship now seems like an empty shell.

Client: Yes, I run over and over in my head why I'm sticking around and the only reasonable answer seems to be guilt. My wife's been a good mother—but that's all she seems to be able to do. She's totally dependent on me. I don't know what she would do without me. She'd be lost. And I feel as though I'm partly responsible for putting her in that position.

Counselor: You're staying to help alleviate that guilt?

Client: Yeah—hell of a reason to stick around. Maybe what I want out of marriage just isn't realistic—maybe lights and bells just aren't supposed to go off anymore.

Counselor: You're beginning to question your expectations about a marriage relationship.

Client: Yeah—I guess that's part of the problem—I'm not sure I'd find anything better with another woman.

Counselor: We've covered a lot of ground today. I know you're still feeling overwhelmed at this point, but I think we've sorted out some starting points that we can work on together. In the work area, we'll begin to identify areas that match your interests, and, as far as the marriage goes, I think a good point that you brought up was for us to begin talking about what you'd like to be getting out of marriage. You may want to begin thinking through which of these areas you'd like to work on first.

Client: Whew—oh—I feel a lot better already, by just beginning to talk about some of these things I've kept bottled up for so long.

Counselor reflects on feelings of hopelessness.

Counselor begins to introduce the concept of disenchantment.

Counselor confronts client.

Counselor begins toward a possible strategy of clarifying expectations.

Counselor summarizes and begins to set goals and asks client to prioritize issues to help structure the next session.

*   *   *

As the client enters the room for an initial interview, the counselor observes that she is an attractive, well-groomed woman of about 45. As she takes a chair, her manner is self-assured.

Interview	Comments

Counselor: Let's start by discussing what we both want and expect from today.

Client: That's just it. I know it's too soon to make plans for my life. Yet my friend Helen insisted that I see you.

Counselor: You feel uneasy about seeing me because your mind is not yet on vocational planning.

Counselor responds to the client's hesitation and her statement that it's too soon to make plans.

(The client then describes the sudden death of her husband, three weeks earlier. Throughout her account, she intersperses comments indicating that her activities have always centered on her husband.)

Counselor: Your grieving is for the loss of the human being you loved and for the loss of your own identity, which was so clearly tied to his.

Client: That's it. Everything I did was so tied to Frank. Everybody who knows me thinks of us and our activities together.

Counselor: You feel frightened about your ability to emerge from this tragedy as a person with your own identity.

Client: I know I'm a person. Yet I don't know exactly how it will emerge. I should tell you about one activity I engaged in separately from Frank. This is really the only time I did something like this. I went to the local political club and was asked to think about taking a part-time job with them. And I was just about to do this when Frank died. Now I don't think I'll go through with it. I really don't know what I'll do now that I have the responsibility for running the family. I just can't think straight. *(She smiles.)* I just thought of something irrelevant. Do you want to hear?

Counselor responds to the client's deep sense of loss, including the loss of some part of herself. This recognition aids further exploration.

The counselor responds to her fear, specifying more clearly the reason for it.

Client points to an aspect of her strength and individuality.

(Counselor nods. The client then describes the night of her husband's death, including the exact time of the phone call that informed her of the death, the clothes she put on, and other apparently trivial details.)

Client: I won't get over this soon.

Counselor: Your grief is overwhelming, and you're confused about whether you should be able to get over it quickly.

Client: I—I can't. I won't, yet I must give my days some meaning.

Counselor: You seem to be telling me some things about yourself. First—and most important—I hear your emptiness and your total feeling of aloneness for a man you loved and who loved you.

Counselor begins to introduce information about "typical" reactions to widowhood. The grieving process can take at least two years and can be very painful.

Counselor tries to abstract and summarize the basic themes that underlie the client's words.

(Client nods.)

Counselor: Then I hear you saying that so much of you was tied up with this man that you're not sure who you are without him. But—and this seems crucial—you've told me about your own emerging individuality.

Counselor points to theme of strength and the eventual goal of counseling: "your own emerging individuality."

Although you have great concerns about who you are, part of you has emerged.

Client: I can't really face looking at the future yet, but deep down I know I'll work something out. What I'd really like to do now is figure out some structure for my days until I am better able to look at the whole picture.

Counselor: You feel partially ready to do some tentative planning.

Client: Partially—that's it. Some days I'm together—like today. But just as quickly something could set me off and I'd be totally dissolved and unable to cope. You know, I'm glad I came to see you. You're the first person who has met me as an individual and not as Frank's wife.

Counselor: You feel pleased about my confirmation of you as an individual.

Client: Yes, it's important to see myself in this new situation.

Counselor: You feel confused because of your need to be seen as an individual in the long run and an even stronger need not to disengage yourself from your long identity as Frank's wife and lover.

Client: You know, my friend Linda did something I didn't like. She brought over a friend of hers who was widowed several years ago. I looked at her and clammed up. I wish Linda had not brought her over. She was so—I don't know—dowdy. I couldn't talk.

Counselor: You felt frightened about the possibility that you might end up sexless and lifeless.

Client: Frank and I had a very full, active life in every regard. I don't want to be like that widow, dead and nobody. I can't imagine life without Frank. I just need something to help me through this horrible time.

Counselor: You referred to the experience you had at the political club. That was your first concrete emerging as an individual involved in your own activities. Would this be a place to start?

Client: I don't know why I hadn't thought of that. The director called me the other day to say how sorry she was. I think that might be a good start. I know everyone there. They know me. I really enjoyed being there and was proud of it. At least I can go out and see about it. But I don't want to go yet. You know, these three weeks seem like an eternity to me. What will the next year be like?

Counselor: You're feeling overwhelmed with despair.

Client: Totally. *(She breathes deeply.)* Yet I don't want to

Client initiates move to the planning stage.

Counselor ignores the client's reference to her inability to cope, feeling that they could return to it: too many raw wounds had already been opened up during the interview.

Counselor tries to give client insight into her fear.

Counselor suggests concrete plan based on client's strengths and previous interest.

leave here until we've talked about some concrete plans.

Counselor: You know you must grieve. You also know that when you're ready to make long-term plans, we can do so. But what you really want is some concrete help about next month.

Client: Yes. Should I do saleswork? I don't even have a B.A. I don't need the money.

Counselor: It's too soon.

Client: Yes. But at least I have something to think about on my good days. I would like to come back and talk again. I feel that you have confidence in me, even meeting me just now.

Counselor: You feel good about our meeting and wonder what I think.

(Client nods affirmatively.)

Counselor: I think you're in for some rough times. It's not easy. It's hell. But I hear a lot of strength and hope and possibility. You have as much adult life ahead as you have behind you. You know it's in your hands. You're afraid. You're thinking: "Can I do it alone? If I don't, will I end up like that other widow hag? What will I become? Yet I'm encouraged because a new person seems to have faith in me. That makes me feel good."

Client: I can't thank you enough.

Counselor summarizes and tries to clarify, weaving in knowledge about the panic that adults often experience when their time perspective shifts and they feel that time is running out.

What the counselors were doing in these two interviews was, first, to reflect the feelings and content of the clients' statements; such responses indicated that the counselors were listening to the clients, understanding their feelings, and empathizing with them. Second, the counselors were relating the clients' particular problems to the larger issues of adult development, thus assuring them that they were not alone with their problems. Third, the counselors were trying to give direction by discussing plans and goals with the clients. In the case of the widow, the counselor suggested short-range goals to get her through the initial period of shock and then alluded to longer-range goals that could be discussed when the client was ready. In the interview with the middle-aged man, the counselor moved toward planning and goal formulation in the areas of career and marriage.

Many books have been written on the counseling process itself. Here we will concentrate on the special components of counseling adults: a knowledge of adult development, and the ability to apply that knowledge; the ability to listen and respond effectively; and a practical understanding of the decision-making process.

In Chapter 2, physical, intellectual, personality, and sex-role development during the adult years were summarized, and recurring developmental issues—including turning points and role changes, stress, stock-taking, shift in time perspective, and locus of control—were outlined. Chapter 3 looked at development in the two main arenas in which adults operate: work and interpersonal relations. In this section, we will indicate how such information may be useful to the counselor in working with adults.

As has been indicated previously, it is commonly believed that adulthood is a period of stability and certainty: that "good" adults make their most important decisions in their 20s and then settle down and follow through on those decisions with a minimum of fuss and difficulty. This "rather cruel illusion" (Levinson et al., 1976, p. 23) leaves many adults unprepared for the changes that they may experience as they move through life. They understand and accept as natural the fears that children feel when confronted with new or unexpected situations—a tonsillectomy, a move to a new town, the first airplane trip alone—but they cannot accept their own negative or confused feelings when confronted with the realization that they have gone as far as they can in their careers and time is running out, or that they have been very successful but their work is boring and meaningless to them, or that having raised children and seen them all safely married is not as satisfying as it should be. And the reason that they cannot accept such feelings is that they do not understand them: they do not understand that such anxieties are as natural and as common among adults as among children.

In addition, many adults feel that it is somewhat shameful to have to ask for outside help in solving their problems. This feeling is heightened by the belief, still prevalent among older people and among people from lower-class backgrounds, that to seek professional help of any kind implies serious psychological disorder. The effective counselor is aware of these feelings, recognizing, for instance, that a 40-year-old returning to college is entering an entirely different situation from that of an 18-year-old enrolling in college for the first time, and that age deviancy—the conviction that one is "off time" —constitutes a major problem for many adults.

The effective counselor knows, too, that although new experiences are a daily occurrence, so to speak, for children, even positive change may constitute a severe stress for adults. As Bocknek (1976) points out, "Any increase in freedom and autonomy is usually accompanied by a dystonic sense of personal isolation and responsibility" (p. 38). A counselor with a knowledge of adult development would be cognizant of this ambivalence and would understand, for instance, why an adult getting a long-hoped-for job promotion or having the opportunity to travel extensively might feel anxious or uncertain as well as exhilarated; a counselor without this knowledge might dismiss such feelings as childish and eccentric.

With a knowledge of adult development, the counselor can "legitimize" the client's feelings and thus reduce anxieties about them. Often, this legitimation requires no more than a few words: "It's understandable how scared you must feel about going back to college"; "Moving to a strange city can be a frightening experience"; "It's not easy to get over the death of a parent; it takes time; be kind to yourself." Such statements assure clients that it is "all right" to feel the way they do, that other people have similar feelings, that they are not alone. Such assurances are prerequisite for developing an adult's ability to cope.

The usefulness of a knowledge of adult development is illustrated by the following example from the area of intimacy and family life. A 35-year-old woman who has been married 12 years and has two children in elementary school tells the counselor that her marriage seems to be on the rocks: The joy of the early years is dead. She is caught up in the daily grind of housework and of chauffeuring her children around to their various activities, while her husband is busy at his job from morning until night. Their interests have diverged; they can no longer communicate; the love has gone out of their marriage. The unsophisticated counselor might jump to the conclusion that the marriage is indeed headed for disaster (as well it may be). But the counselor who knows something about the pattern of a typical marriage may reach a different, and tentative, conclusion. As mentioned in Chapter 3, married couples at different stages of the family life course define their marriages in dramatically different ways (Thurnher, 1975). Newlyweds describe the unique qualities of their partners, their close communication and special relationship. When children are born, traditional marriages become defined by roles, with the mother parenting and the father providing; it is during this period that the greatest dissatisfaction occurs. After the children leave home, however, there is often a resurgence of happiness (Bernard, 1972, p. 63). As couples move into the preretirement stage, they evidence a "renewed interest in the personalities of their spouses" (Thurnher, 1975, p. 25). A knowledge of this typical developmental pattern does not mean that the counselor should interpret all marital difficulties as part of this evolving relationship, but it does serve as a framework within which both client and counselor can interpret a particular marriage.

Finally, knowledge of adult development can be helpful in anticipating the major transitions of adulthood. Lowenthal and Pierce (1975) found that "the sense of inner control was clearly the most important of the pretransitional cognitions, being strongly associated with a positive attitude toward the transition, as well as with planning for it" (p. 209). Thus, the counselor who knows what kinds of transitions adults are likely to go through, and what feelings are likely to accompany such transitions, can help clients understand and plan for the transition, thus enabling them to develop an inner locus of control.

EFFECTIVE LISTENING AND RESPONDING

It is a truism that effective listening and responding are the essentials of good counseling. Not only do they build rapport and open lines of communication between counselor and client, but also they help to keep the counselor's biases in check. To truly listen to the client is to be tuned in to his or her perspective, to look behind the social mask and see the real person, to share momentarily the client's own values and hopes. Adults repeatedly state that understanding and support are the crucial elements they seek when they come to a counselor. Often the first few minutes of a counseling interview can tell them whether these elements are present.

What can counselors do to demonstrate their understanding and support? We can listen as accurately and completely as possible and formulate responses that are as nonjudgmental as possible. We can "hear the subtext" of the clients' words, inferring what is left unsaid from what is said. We can reinforce clients in the often difficult task of talking to someone about their hopes, uncertainties, and fears.

All very well and good, you may say, but exactly how does one go about actualizing these very laudable intentions? The activities outlined in Chapter 9 are designed to give you practice in the skills of effective listening and responding. What is presented in this section will serve as a background to those activities.

Carkhuff and Berenson (1967) have developed a counseling model that specifies three sequential goals: (1) self-exploration, (2) self-understanding, and (3) action and directionality. The sample interviews that opened this chapter demonstrate this approach. In the self-exploration phase, the counselor tried to respond empathically and accurately to the client, reflecting both the feeling and the content of the client's words, listening for key words and repeating or rephrasing them. The self-understanding aspect of the interviews lay in the counselor's relating the client's specific problems to the larger developmental issues, generalizing from the particular, abstracting the "theme." The third phase—action and directionality—was necessarily brief in the first interview, but the goal of planning was clearly introduced.

The rationale for the self-exploration stage is that, "to be creative in all spheres of endeavor, including the interpersonal" (Carkhuff & Berenson, 1967, p. 224), people must be able to "experience" themselves. The counselor makes this possible by reflecting back the feeling and content of the client's words.

Consider the following exchange, a statement by a client followed by four possible alternative responses:

> *Client:* Sometimes I get so depressed I just don't know what to do.
> *Counselor #1:* Everybody feels that way once in a while; you'll get over it.
> *Counselor #2:* You spend too much time brooding about yourself.
> *Counselor #3:* When was the last time you felt depressed?
> *Counselor #4:* Sometimes you feel so down that it's almost impossible to function.

The first response undercuts the client by belittling the feelings expressed: the counselor is saying, in effect, "Your depression isn't important enough to spend time talking about; it's just a passing mood." The counselor has failed to empathize with the client. The second response is obviously judgmental: the counselor is preaching at the client, making a negative appraisal that reveals a lack of understanding and support. The third response raises an irrelevant question and is, moreover, interrogative in tone. Only the fourth response reflects with accuracy the feeling and content of the client's words, at the same time implying respect for the client's right to feel depressed.

Another example to consider is the following:

> *Client:* Hey, I've always wanted to finish my high school diploma, but being 40 and having four kids to support makes it really rough. Do you think I'm crazy to even think about it?
> *Counselor #1:* Have you looked into taking the G.E.D. exam?
> *Counselor #2:* It sounds as though you're trying to decide what's really important to you.
> *Counselor #3:* It doesn't sound as though a high school diploma will do anything for you at your age.
> *Counselor #4:* Why would you want the diploma anyway?

Which of these counselor responses is the most effective? Why?

During the initial, self-exploratory phase, counselors may find it difficult not to minimize the client's feelings by reducing them to a generalization or a formula ("Everybody feels that way once in a while"), not to display superior knowledge or coping ability, not to impose their own values on the client. As a check on these tendencies, the counselor should make frequent use of the formula "You feel . . . because" or simply "You feel that. . . ."

Another way that counselors can check their tendency to give inappropriate responses is to "rehearse" their responses through the process of self-verbalization. Before responding (whether in a counseling interview or in ordinary conversation), we all indulge in a kind of interior monologue, a subvocalization of our own thoughts and feelings. Usually, we are unaware of this monologue because it takes place in a split second. Several investigators (Meichenbaum, 1973; Ochiltree, Brekke, & Yager, 1975) have explored the feasibility of making this process more conscious and more explicit as a self-instructional modeling approach in learning to empathize and to communicate. This approach calls upon counselors to ask themselves six questions before responding to the client: (1) What is the client expressing, verbally and nonverbally? (2) What do I really feel about what a person of that age should do? (3) How would I feel if I were in his or her place? (4) What would I really like to say? (5) What is wrong with that response? (6) What will I say: what is the least biased, most effective response I can give? By answering these questions—at first, in practice, out loud and then, as the process becomes more automatic, subvocally—counselors can focus on the self-verbalization process and eventually learn to make more effective responses. (This technique, with exemplary activities, is dealt with more thoroughly in Chapter 9.)

Conscious use of self-verbalization is especially helpful during the self-understanding phase of counseling. After reflecting the feeling and content, thus making it possible for clients to "experience themselves," the counselor must next go beyond the immediate material and help clients put the pieces together. To do so, the counselor must be able to hear not only the obvious cues about thoughts and feelings—the client's direct expression—but also the "subtext." The term *subtext* is borrowed from method acting, where it is used to refer to what is going on in a character underneath the words that are said—the thoughts, feelings, and motives that lie behind a speech. The concept is useful for the actor or actress in building a character and may be equally useful to the counselor in listening to a client.

In the second sample interview at the beginning of the chapter, the counselor recognized that, although the client was expressing genuine grief over the loss of her husband, she was also expressing anxiety about herself: Could she make it as a person in her own right? Did she have a distinct identity? But the client was asking these questions only indirectly, when she mentioned that everything she did was closely tied to her husband, that they shared the same activities, that everyone thought of them as a pair. The counselor heard the subtext under these comments and could respond, "You feel frightened about your ability to emerge from this tragedy as a person with your own identity." Similarly, when the client talked about being offered a part-time job by the local political club, she was also asserting her own strength and competence. The counselor heard the subtext and was able to return to the point later on in the interview.

To take another example: A 45-year-old man complains to the counselor that his son, a high school senior, is "turning out badly"—not living up to the hopes and expectations that his parents have for him. The boy seems uninterested in going to college, talks about joining a commune and living close to the earth, is totally absorbed with his friends, no longer talks to his parents. The counselor's initial reaction might be simply to label this an example of the "generation gap." But this label, like most labels, is superficial and does not help to get to the heart of the problem. The counselor who hears the subtext will recognize that, in part at least, the client is grieving for his own lost youth and dreams, that he has transferred some of his aspirations to his son. Citing the work of Levinson and his associates, Brim (1976) says:

A man during his children's adolescence must inevitably compare a fantasy, his belief in his own power and influence to mold his child into some ideal being, with what is now becoming a reality, and accept the limited nature of his own influence. This reconciliation of aspirations to reality is likely to take place at the same time that his occupational aspiration-achievement gap is being worked through [p. 6].

To hear the subtext requires that counselors be familiar with the issues of adult development, as discussed in the previous section, and also that they focus on the third question in the self-verbalization process: "How would I feel if I were in his/her place?" Or, to put it slightly differently, "If I were to say these words, what would I be feeling/thinking?"

To return to the Carkhuff/Berenson model: In the self-understanding phase of the counseling process, the counselor goes beyond reflecting the client's feeling and content to make "additive responses"—summarizing the underlying theme of the client's words and, where necessary, pointing out discrepancies between the client's statements of wants or goals and the client's actions. As the client reaches a new level of self-understanding, the final phase, that of action or directionality, begins. It is at this point that the counselor requires a knowledge of the decision-making process.

THE CENTRALITY OF DECISION MAKING

As has been stated repeatedly, adulthood today is usually a period of change more than stability. Adults pass through a series of transitions, taking on new roles or losing old ones, forming new networks of relationships, sometimes even changing their self-definitions. Some of the changes of adulthood are general (though not universal) and predictable: getting a job, getting married, having children, retiring. Others may be idiosyncratic: getting divorced, changing careers in mid-life. Some

changes are deliberate and planned: moving to a new city, returning to school. Others are unexpected and beyond the control of the individual: the death of a spouse, the loss of a job. But whatever the nature of the change, it usually entails, at some point, making a decision.

Indeed, one is constantly making decisions—usually several decisions at the same time, though most are relatively minor. Even those people who lack a sense of inner control, who feel that their lives are controlled by external forces, are in effect making a decision by taking such a stance. The decision not to act, out of apathy and passivity, is nonetheless a decision. The issue is how to make decisions that are as informed and rational as possible. And many people lack the skills to make such decisions.

It should be emphasized that the function of the counselor is not to force the client to move in a particular direction or to choose one particular option over others: the choice and responsibility are the client's. The function of the counselor is to help the client understand the decision-making process; to liberate the client as much as possible from artificial constraints imposed by cultural norms based on extraneous factors such as sex, social class, racial/ethnic background, and age; and to enable the client to establish an internal locus of control. Specifically, the counselor's task is twofold: defining where the client is in the decision-making process, and suggesting strategies that will facilitate the client's movement through the process.

A Decision-Making Model

Tiedeman and O'Hara (1963) present a decision-making model that has proved useful in counseling. As Figure 4-1 indicates, all decisions have two stages: *anticipation* and *implementation*. Each of these stages comprises two substages.

The first substage in the anticipatory stage is

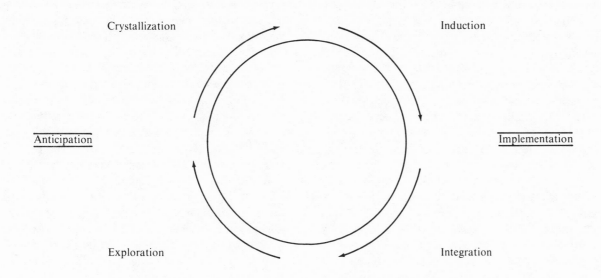

Crystallization   Induction

Anticipation   Implementation

Exploration   Integration

Process Is Repeated

FIGURE 4-1. The decision-making process. (Adapted from *Career Development: Choice and Adjustment,* by D. V. Tiedeman and R. P. O'Hara. Copyright 1963 by College Entrance Examination Board. Reprinted by permission.)

exploration, which has two aspects: self-exploration, including clarifying values, assessing interests, and identifying skills; and exploration of the area in which the decision is to be made, including developing alternatives, gathering information on these alternatives, and assessing the probable outcomes of various alternatives. Gradually, one enters into the second substage, *crystallization:* patterns emerge, some possibilities are discarded, and the options are narrowed down. Finally, a choice is made, and then one organizes to implement that choice.

In the second major stage, implementation, one first moves into the new situation *(induction).* At this point, the orientation is primarily receptive

—a willingness to accommodate to the perceived expectations of others. As one gains confidence in the new situation or role and comes to be accepted by others, one becomes more assertive and gradually enters into the final substage, *integration.*

The first substage of the entire process—exploration—is obviously important, in that it determines everything that follows. If one is too timid during the exploration phase, whole areas of possibilities are cut off, and the future becomes unnecessarily restricted. One of the reasons that, until recently, very few women have become outstanding physical scientists or top business executives is that at no point in their lives were they encouraged to explore or even consider these possibilities. If an entire group limits its fantasies to getting married, having children, and keeping house— or to going into one of a very limited number of occupations such as nursing, teaching, or office work—then that is where most of the group will end up. What is true for women is equally true for other subgroups within the larger population, especially racial/ethnic minorities. Indeed, the occupational clustering of any subgroup can be examined in terms of the dreams that these subgroups allow themselves to have or are encouraged to have.

The counselor, then, should encourage clients to explore widely and even wildly during the anticipatory stage, should stimulate their fantasizing and dreaming, should suggest possibilities they may never have considered. Only after such freewheeling exploration has taken place should they go on to the next stage. Eventually, the client will narrow down the choices in accordance with his or her own capabilities and values; but the crystallization will be very different for the adult who has fantasized about a variety of options than it is for the adult who, from the beginning, has viewed his or her future as given. The more options one entertains, the more likely it is that the final choice will be closer to one's true desires.

In addition to encouraging exploration, the counselor can help the client obtain information about various options and to evaluate them. In the area of career decisions, for instance, the counselor can guide clients to sources of information on various occupations, their requirements and rewards. (Chapter 8 lists organizations that might be contacted for information that will help the client with different kinds of decisions; Chapter 9 includes a number of activities that will guide the client in this stage of the process.)

But anticipation is only half the battle; the other half, implementation, remains to be fought.

Unfortunately, society often erects unnecessary barriers to implementation, most obviously in the vocational area. For instance, the 36-year-old man who decides that he wants to become a dentist can do little to implement that choice if schools of dentistry decree that age 35 is the cutoff point for admission. The woman who wants to become a jockey but is aware of the difficulty that women have in getting into that occupational field may hesitate to act upon her choice. Even the person who gets past the conventional barriers and is inducted into the new system may find that the hostility of others makes integration difficult. For instance, the woman who is hired as the first female attorney in a law firm may find herself patronized or ignored by her male colleagues. What can the counselor do to help clients who face problems such as these in reaching their goals?

Let it be acknowledged at the outset that counseling is no panacea for the world's ills; it cannot solve all the problems faced by adults. In periods when unemployment is high, for instance, it may be difficult to find any job at all, let alone a job that provides personal gratification and fulfillment. To take an example from another area: Some people may be in family situations that simply cannot be changed in any basic way, however constricting and frustrating they may be. Thus, in some cases, goals must be scaled down to meet realities. Some of the specific kinds of help with implementation that the counselor can offer, however, include guiding the client in action planning, helping the client to get assertiveness training and to become more proficient in job-finding skills, and suggesting support groups that the client might join (see Chapter 9). In some cases, the counselor may be moved to take social action, a third type of intervention discussed in "A Final Word" and mentioned in some of the examples that follow.

Application of the Decision-Making Model

The first step in applying this model to the problems of adult clients is to determine just where a particular client is in the decision-making process. The distinction between exploration and implementation is often not easy to make. The counselor cannot always take the client's word for it but, again, must try to hear the subtext.

To illustrate: One of the authors recently received a telephone call from a 36-year-old man, a stranger, who had heard that she was conducting research on mid-life career change among adult men. He explained that he worked as an insurance agent but had decided to become a lawyer. What law school would she suggest he apply to? On the face of it, this is an implementation question. But something about the way he asked the question suggested that he was much more tentative than he sounded. He was really saying "I'm confused, I'm unhappy with my job, I want a change. Is it too late to make that change? What should I do?" The reason he asked an implementation question was his feeling that his lack of certainty was "unmanly." Therefore, in her role as counselor, the author focused on exploration, reflecting the feeling of his statement by suggesting that possibly he was experiencing a sense of panic that time was running out. This comment was greeted with relief by the caller, who immediately agreed that he was uncertain and frightened about the future. After some discussion on the issue of the change in time perspective, the man was silent for a moment or two. Then he said that he wanted to think some more and that he would call the counselor back later. That conversation began a process of painful self-exploration that lasted for several months.

The following case, which was presented to one of the authors in an industrial setting, also illustrates the need to differentiate between anticipation and implementation questions.

> A 40-year-old man came into the counselor's office and quickly stated that he was looking for a new job. He had just completed a degree in business after many years of part-time school, and now he wanted to be able to use his newly acquired degree. The counselor spent a few minutes talking about the kind of work he wanted to do, and she quickly sensed that he wasn't really anxious to talk about future possibilities. She redirected the session and began to ask about the work he was presently doing. In response, she got a 10-minute enthusiastic description of his work as an engineering technician. Further probing in this direction revealed that he really liked what he was doing and didn't want to change but felt pressure to formally use his degree. He felt that the whole degree would be wasted if he couldn't apply it in a new job. It was this kind of thinking that had led him to the counselor's office. The counselor began to help him explore these thoughts of "having to" change jobs. She suggested that, instead of looking for an entirely new job, they try to identify parts of his present job where he could apply what he had learned in school. This strategy was enthusiastically received, and the man commented that some of his feelings of guilt and of wasting his degree were alleviated.

An inexperienced counselor might have jumped to the strategy of looking for a new job, rather than exploring some of the more salient issues. As a result, the counselor might have been confused or frustrated when the client did not respond to her suggestions in that area.

Let's consider a different kind of case. The client talking is a 34-year-old woman:

> I graduated from college and was on my way to a career as a playwright. I met an exciting man who is now an outstanding scientist. We fell in love—

that is, we loved to be together. We loved to talk, to dream, to make love. We were alive and felt the world was our oyster. After we married, nothing tarnished. Our sex life was better than ever, our talks more meaningful. "What's this talk about unhappy, meaningless marriages?" we wondered. Then I got pregnant. And believe it or not, I had twins. Two years later, I had a third child. Suddenly, I was catapulted into a world I hadn't chosen —diapers, laundry, scrubbing floors, doctors, shopping, cooking, cleaning, and over and over again. Suddenly I was overwhelmed with the mechanics of living, while Bob continued in his world of science and esoteric academic living. Of course, I made him pay. I screamed and tortured him at nights. So much so that he started working late two or three nights a week. Sex became a horror to endure. My skin was too tense and aching to be touched. And worst of all I felt guilty because I knew I should be a good wife and mother and had no right to feel this way.

Is this woman at the anticipation or the implementation stage of decision making? Is she concerned with making a decision at all, and if so, about what: herself as an individual, her interpersonal relations with her husband and children, her job as a homemaker?

The counselor in this case encouraged the woman to focus more by responding with interest but without value judgment. The more the woman talked and was listened to, the more her dilemma was legitimized, and the better able she was to understand and to define her situation. Though at first she seemed unhappy about everything in her life, it soon became clear that there were only some aspects she wanted to change. The nightmarish quality of her situation was caused primarily by her feeling that she had no control over her life, that she was a pawn being pushed around by her husband and children. Soon she came to recognize that her situation was partly of her own making, in that she was trying to live up to her own strict rules

about the proper behavior for a wife and mother— rules that said husband and children come first, no matter what. This self-imposed demand became the first focus of exploration, and she, with the help of the counselor, began to search for less stringent rules by which she could run her life. That she was the one who could make or change the rules gave her a sense of mastery over her own fate.

To implement the preliminary decision to change the rules, the counselor helped her to form a "rap group" with other women in similar situations and agreed to act as leader and moderator. As the woman moved toward greater autonomy and a new self-identification, she found that she could not reestablish her earlier intimate relation with her husband, and after two years of trying to work out their marital problems, the couple divorced. The client then began to explore other ways of managing her life. With the counselor's help, she found nursery schools and day-care centers for her children, arranged for part-time help and for meal-sharing with neighbors, and eventually set up a studio at home and established a schedule that included a set time for writing. It proved more difficult to implement her plans than to define them, but she was more fortunate than many women in similar circumstances, in that she had already completed her education and did not have to consider returning to school for further training; she received enough support from her ex-husband so that she did not have to take paid employment; and she found a house that was small enough to be easy to manage but had a small room that she could use as an office. As an added bit of good fortune, the local theater group produced one of her earlier plays. Without this encouragement, she might have needed more counseling to help her explore other avenues for creative achievement, so that she could get the reward of recognition that she so desperately needed.

Most of the cases discussed so far exemplify vocational decisions at the entry level. Decision making at later stages and in other areas may also present problems. Consider the following cases:

A man of 62, recently retired from a job in business, found that he and his wife were no longer compatible. They had stayed together for 40 years "for the sake of the children," but now that the children were grown, and now that he no longer had a job to occupy him, their life together had become difficult and unpleasant. Should they get divorced, or perhaps just separate? Unfortunately, he could find no one who would listen to his marital problems: his minister just laughed patronizingly and said something about "old dogs."

A priest came to a counselor with the lament that "I'm 49 years old and at a crossroads. I've been a priest for 25 years and in my role as a priest I've had administrative and supervisory responsibilities. I'm also interested in a woman and I'm also rethinking my career. I need some assistance in this rethinking." It was clear to the counselor that he was asking exploratory questions. The counselor decided that the most effective strategy would be to help him clarify some of these issues before actual decisions were made and acted upon.

A couple in their 40s, somewhat uncomfortable and embarrassed, told a counselor that they were concerned about the mental health of the husband's mother and wanted some advice on what they should do about her. In the year since she had been widowed, the mother—always overbearing and difficult to get along with—had increased her many demands on her three children, particularly on the client and on his sister, who had finally moved to another city 2500 miles away just to escape from the problem. Listening to the couple describe the mother's domineering personality and introduce the possibility that she needed special treatment and should perhaps be placed in a nursing home, the counselor wondered why they were considering such placement now, when the mother's behavior was no different from what it had always been. She was in good health and managed

her business and personal affairs competently. It seemed illogical to treat her as deteriorating and more logical to focus on the feelings of the clients about their interaction with her. The counselor began probing other possibilities: How could they respond when the mother (who could drive and had her own car) demanded that they take her shopping, for example? Would they be interested in family therapy that involved the mother, the client and his wife, and perhaps the client's younger brother? The couple seemed somewhat surprised by these suggestions; they had thought of the mother's problems in terms of her old age, not as long-standing personality problems, and so could come up with only the stereotyped solution of putting her in a nursing home. They agreed to discuss the question with the other siblings and, at the very least, to encourage the mother to develop outside interests and to seek counseling for her loneliness.

A single woman in her early 50s, moderately successful as a public relations officer for a small East Coast firm, received an attractive job offer from a Los Angeles company. She sought counseling because she was having difficulty deciding whether to accept the offer (which would have meant a more responsible position at a better salary) or to stay where she was, with a large circle of friends and an established position in the community. This woman was at the exploratory stage, but her search was not for new options; what she needed was guidelines that would help her to evaluate her existing options.

Another woman of 54, who had worked as an administrative assistant before her marriage but had then dropped out of the world of work for 30 years to devote herself to running a household and raising five children, decided to go back to work again when her youngest child entered college. But she had no idea what she wanted to do. She came to a counselor, and together they began exploring options and narrowing down choices. The woman decided that she was not interested in a job that would require her returning to school first. Though her academic training was long outdated, she had in her years out of the labor force developed her managerial and interpersonal skills, not only through her homemaking activities but also through volunteer work in community organizations. She wanted a job where she could put these skills to immediate use. Having clarified her interests, she set about making inquiries, and in the course of talking to some acquaintances, she heard that the local hospital was looking for someone who could coordinate the work of the secretaries and provide the kind of comforting yet practical presence desired with patients and families facing medical crises. She applied for the position, was hired, and proved highly effective; moreover, she was able to adjust the hours so that she could still perform sporadic duties as wife and mother.

Conclusion

Making decisions is a continuous process in adult life. Adults seek out counselors for various ostensible reasons, but most client problems can be analyzed within a decision-making framework. Feelings of boredom, depression, panic that time is running out, despair over inability to communicate with other people—all indicate a desire to change one's life structure, however undefined that desire may be. By viewing problems within this framework, the counselor is given a definite starting point from which to work and can suggest strategies for action; clients can thereby perceive a definite sense of direction in their lives and, moreover, can assume responsibility for that direction. Thus, the locus of control can be shifted from the external to the internal.

For activities and skills related to this chapter, see Chapter 9.

5

Interventions: Focus on Program Planning

As stated in the previous chapter, the chief mode of intervention is the counseling activity itself: dealing with clients directly, either on an individual basis or in a group. But this mode has its limitations. First, the client must generally take the initiative in seeking out the counselor. Many adults may be unwilling to acknowledge that they need help and thus may fail to take advantage of the help available to them. More frequently, they are unaware that such help exists, and counselors must make special efforts to reach them. Recently, the number of state and local agencies (for example, employment services, industry counseling, community mental health services) has increased, and new programs are constantly being developed (see Harrison & Entine, 1976); but these, like academic vocational guidance services, are not known to most people.

THE NEED FOR ADULT COUNSELING PROGRAMS

In 1970, about 46% of all Americans were between 25 and 65 years old. This age group comprises a large number of people who may need and

want counseling in various areas of their lives. Many adults, undergoing stress in their interpersonal or intrapersonal lives—including widows and widowers, the separated and divorced, the handicapped, the unemployed—do not know where to turn for appropriate help, particularly if they are isolated from family and friends, geographically or psychologically. In short, many people must cope with stress and make decisions in a vacuum, deprived of the kind of help that they may desperately require.

For simplicity, let us limit our consideration to people faced with educational and career decisions who might be helped by counseling but who ordinarily do not have such services available to them. Such people might include high school and college dropouts, transfer students, veterans of military service, women planning to reenter the job market, adults considering mid-career shifts, and retired people trying to find some meaningful activity to fill their time.

Data are hard to come by on some of these groups—women wanting to reenter the labor force, adults wanting to change careers, retired people wanting second careers—but some idea of their

75

numbers can be gained by the indirect evidence of adult education enrollment figures. According to the American Personnel and Guidance Association (1974), one of every 50 men and women 35 or older is going back to school, most of them on a part-time basis. If these adults represent the proportion of people who have been successful in continuing their education, how many more adults must there be in the population who would probably return if they had adequate counseling? It seems reasonable to conclude that large numbers want to consider some kind of job or lifestyle change. Clearly, a genuine need exists to build programs that will systematically link adults with available resources.

The question remains: where should these programs be located? One setting that has become increasingly responsive to the counseling needs of adults is the workplace, whether in industry or in government. In Chapter 4, we described a case in which a middle-aged man was experiencing feelings of despair in his work and marriage. Many industrial and government agencies are beginning to recognize the fact that many of their employees may have similar concerns. Several of these agencies have tried to develop programs that include individual counseling, workshops, seminars, and short-term rotational job assignments. Programs such as these exist at Goddard Space Flight Center, Greenbelt, Maryland; Lawrence Livermore Laboratories, Livermore, California; and the Mitre Corporation, McLean, Virginia.

Program design can start with only a small proportion of the population of clients who have sought out the counselor. The effective program designer uses his/her experience with this small proportion as the basis for building a program that will help others in the same population. In Chapter 4, for example, we observed a case in which the counselor sought to give support and assurance to a middle-aged woman whose husband had recently died. Specifically, the counselor tried to help the woman explore her own feelings of loss, grief, and anxiety; to gain a deeper understanding of the sources of these feelings (in particular, the fear that she had lost a part of herself, that her identity had been destroyed by the death of her husband); to marshal her resources for coping with these feelings; and to give her some direction, some sense of control in planning her own life. But this process helped only that one woman. What about the many women—and men as well—who may be widowed relatively young and who may not seek professional help? What can the counselor do, in the role of program planner, to reach this population?

One answer might be the design of a series of workshops for widows, to include lectures by various experts on coping with some of the problems of bereavement—not just the problems of dealing with the welter of feelings that accompany the death of a spouse, but more practical problems such as how to arrange one's life, how to plan for the future, how to handle day-to-day exigencies such as financial management, keeping house, caring for children, and other responsibilities that may have previously been the domain of the spouse. The counselor would have to consider carefully the particular group at whom the program was aimed. For instance, it seems likely that widows and widowers would face somewhat different problems, so the workshop might be limited to one sex or the other. In addition, younger adults, who have been widowed unexpectedly, are probably under more stress and encounter a somewhat different range of difficulties than do older adults, who have rehearsed for widowhood. To reach the potential clientele for such workshops, the program planner may have to step beyond the usual channels for publicizing counseling services—perhaps by posting notices on the bulletin boards of local supermarkets and of the public library. The success of a program depends to a considerable extent on the imagination and energy of its designer.

Though virtually all counselors engage in program planning at some point in their careers, they usually do so on an ad hoc basis, without having had specific training in this aspect of counseling. It is perhaps impossible to do away entirely with the trial-and-error aspect in program planning. A certain amount of guesswork, testing, and revision seems inevitable. However sensitive and experienced the person planning the program, he/she will not be able to foresee all the contingencies and special problems that will arise in dealing with a particular group of adults.

A poignant example of the difficulties that may be encountered comes from an account by Robert Weiss (1976) of his experience in trying to develop Seminars for the Bereaved modeled after Seminars for the Separated, an earlier program that had proved highly effective in helping people recently separated or divorced. Weiss soon found that, although both groups had lost their spouses, the nature of the loss—and the feelings that it evoked—were so dissimilar as to make the methods that had worked with the first group entirely inappropriate for the second group. For instance, the separated had found it helpful to hear lectures on, and to discuss among themselves, the nature and impact of their emotions; they were often bewildered and confused by the ambivalence of these feelings and so were reassured to learn that others in the same position felt the same way and that the feelings (such as continued attachment to the estranged spouse) could be explained. In contrast, lectures on the nature and impact of their emotions were extremely painful to the bereaved: they did not need anyone to tell them the reasons for their feelings, and they derived no benefit from having those feelings reawakened. Moreover, they had less rapport with and sympathy for other members of the group whose circumstances were very different from their own and tended to feel resentful of discussion. In short, what worked for one group simply did not work for the other; but the program planner had no way of knowing this until it was actually tried out. Weiss (1976) concludes:

> Unfortunately, it appears that the only way we can develop an effective program for the bereaved—or, indeed, for those in any distress-inducing situation —is by trial and error. Our assumptions and anticipations are too often imprecise or mistaken for us to develop an effective program from them alone [pp. 224–225].*

Despite these uncertainties, the problem of program design can be approached systematically, drawing on tested procedures from social psychology. The next section outlines some of the steps.

THE PROCESS OF PROGRAM DESIGN

The model that is presented here is eclectic, adapted from several sources including Weiss (1976), Fox, Lippitt, and Schindler-Rainman (1975), and the American Institutes for Research (1975). We have not attempted to give a comprehensive view of the approach proposed by each of these sources but rather have tried to select from each the particular points that seemed to us most practical for the reader. Thus, we will emphasize the following four phases: (1) defining the target group; (2) identifying specific objectives; (3) designing and selecting strategies; and (4) evaluating the program.

*From "Transition States and Other Stressful Situations: Their Nature and Programs for Their Management," by R. S. Weiss. In G. Caplan and M. Killilea (Eds.), *Support Systems and Mutual Help: Multidisciplinary Explorations.* Copyright 1976 by Grune & Stratton, Inc. Reprinted by permission.

The first phase actually involves three steps. The counselor must (a) select a target group, (b) define that group as precisely as possible, and (c) assess the particular needs of the group.

Selecting the group for which one will design a program depends in part on the counselor's own interests and experience, in part upon the particular organization for which the counselor works, and in part upon the needs of the population of the particular locale in which the counselor is based. For instance, a program designed to help minority-group members improve job-seeking skills might be appropriate in an inner-city area where unemployment runs high; a program designed to help middle-class women facing the postparental period explore and develop their interests might be appropriate in an affluent suburb; a program designed to introduce foreigners to American culture might be appropriate at an academic institution that enrolls large numbers of foreign students or in a neighborhood with large numbers of immigrants.

Having decided on the target group, the program planner must next define that group as precisely as possible (see the Form for Analyzing the Population in Chapter 8). What is likely to be the sex composition of the group if the program is one directed at both men and women? What is likely to be its racial/ethnic composition? What is likely to be the age range or the stage of development? What is likely to be the socioeconomic composition (including educational background) of the group? In some cases, answers to these questions may be inherent in the selection of a particular group, as in the example above of a program for middle-class women facing the postparental period. In other cases, the group may be more heterogeneous with respect to the demographic and background characteristics listed above. But the program designer

will probably have to engage in some speculation—and research—about these characteristics in order to design specific strategies.

For instance, a program planner interested in designing a program for adults making major career changes would be helped by knowing that interest in such changes is strongest among the widowed and divorced and among white-collar workers; that there is a distinction between people simply interested in making a change and those actually engaged in making a change, the former group tending to be less educated than the latter; and that people making major career changes must often take sharp cuts in salary (Pascal, 1975). The program developer interested in designing a program for women enrolled in continuing education classes would be helped by knowing that, according to one recent study, members of this group are likely to be white, well-educated, and married to men in business or professional occupations, and that the median age is 36 (Astin, 1976). The statistics in both these examples are national, and the program designer would probably need to have figures relating to a particular locale. For instance, it seems likely that a fairly large proportion of women returning to school in urban areas would be minority-group members.

After defining the general characteristics of the group, the program developer should make some effort to assess the particular needs that the program is designed to meet. For instance, people interested in making mid-career changes may be uncertain about their own interests, values, and skills, and they may be uninformed about career options and the current job market. Women returning to school may feel out of place among younger students, may lack study skills, or may have difficulties arranging for child care while they are in classes. These are definite needs that might be met through programs of different kinds. Another point is that people require different kinds of help or intervention depending on what kind of stressful situation they are undergoing.

Weiss (1976) offers a useful way of classifying different types of *situational distress,* defined as "reactions that are so much the product of exposure to a particular situation that they are displayed by almost everyone in the situation" (p. 213). The first, which Weiss labels a *crisis,* is a sudden, severely upsetting situation of short duration that requires the individual to mobilize his/her energies and resources. (Note that Weiss uses the term more restrictively than it is ordinarily used, in this book and elsewhere.) An example of a crisis in this sense is an accident or the sudden onset of a major illness in the family. People in crisis are frequently emotionally numbed; their feelings are suspended.

Then the crisis passes, and the situation either returns to normal or ends in change. Either the family member returns to the former state of health, or else the relative dies or is permanently invalided. In the latter case, the affected individual enters a *transition state.* This period is marked by relational and personal changes, including attempts to deal with upset, grief, and other disruptive emotions and to find new sources of support. This period is often marked by confusion and uncertainty as the person attempts to rearrange his/her life. People in transition states are particularly likely to benefit from counseling help, because the decisions they make at this point could profoundly affect the course of the rest of their lives.

The end of a transition state is usually marked by a new life organization and personal identity. The new life situation is either satisfactory or not; if it is not satisfactory, then the individual enters into a *deficit situation.* For example, a widow or widower may find that she or he has continuous difficulty in raising dependent children single-handed, without the aid of another adult. In contrast to a crisis, which is short-lived, a deficit situation tends to be long-lasting.

To individuals experiencing a crisis, support seems to be the only effective kind of help. The helper, who may or may not be a professional person, communicates empathy, understanding, and a readiness to provide whatever service is possible to help the individual through the crisis. Such support is also helpful to those in transition states and deficit situations, but they can benefit as well from other kinds of help.

People in transition must find new ways of managing their lives; thus, they may be helped by cognitive materials that will provide a framework for understanding the new situation. For instance, the new widow or widower may need help in managing finances or in locating child-care services. In addition, people in transition states may be grappling with emotions that they do not understand; thus, they may also be helped by cognitive materials that give them some understanding of their emotions. Support groups may also be useful to those in transition states. The bereaved may find that the social network they shared with the dead spouse gradually disappears and that they are socially isolated. Becoming acquainted with other people in the same situation as themselves may be of practical as well as psychological value, as mutual problems and possible solutions are shared.

People in deficit situations have reached a new period of stability, even if it is unsatisfactory. Short-term help is of little value to them. They need a continuing, problem-focused support system. For instance, parents left single by death or divorce may require continued help with the problems they encounter in trying to raise children on their own.

Both the mid-life career changers and the women returning to education can be classified as people in transition states (though note that, in these cases, the transition need not have been preceded by a crisis, in Weiss's sense of the word). Both groups could profit from support and from exposure to cognitive materials that will help them to adjust to the new situation and to make well-considered, rational decisions.

Identifying Specific Objectives

The next phase of program design is to define the specific objectives of the program: where should the group be when the program is completed? At first, the goals can be stated in abstract terms. For instance, the National Aeronautics and Space Administration, Goddard Space Flight Center, defining as its target group mid-level employees who indicated a desire to make a career change, set up a program with the general goal of exploring new career options. A resource center in Rhode Island, with funding from the National Institute of Education, decided to focus on a population of housebound adults with the general goal of helping them restructure their lives. A program designed for women returning to education might have the general goal of adjustment to the role of college student.

Within the framework of the general goal or purpose, the program planner should gradually develop specific objectives, stated in action terms. For instance, in the Goddard Space Flight Center program, the specific objective would be stated as: to enable mid-level employees to try out different work options through a short-term work experience in a new area. In Rhode Island, the specific objective was: to help adults explore meaningful career activities that can be carried out at home. A program designed for women returning to school might have any (or all) of several specific objectives: to enable women to feel more comfortable in the role of student; to train women in developing study skills; to suggest solutions to some of the difficulties involved in combining the role of student with those of wife and mother; to help women with career planning. The specification of objectives will be useful not only in suggesting possible strategies but also in evaluating the effectiveness of the program.

Designing and Selecting Strategies

Three different types of strategies will be considered. The first two, following Weiss's model, are support and cognitive framework. The third is planning, an important consideration in enabling people to take control of their lives. (Activities connected with designing and selecting strategies are presented in Chapter 10.)

As was pointed out, people undergoing any of the three kinds of situational distress—those in crisis, those in a transition state, and those in a deficit situation—can benefit from support. This support can come in several forms. An individual who empathizes with the feelings experienced by the person in distress and who indicates that he or she is willing to help in any way possible can provide support. That individual can be either an expert (such as a counselor) or a veteran (someone who has experienced the same situation at some point in the past and has weathered it). Presence of a veteran may in itself be a hopeful sign that people do survive stress and make successful transitions.

Support can also be given by a group of people who are in the same situation. Adults need assurance that they are not alone in their feelings, particularly if those feelings are somewhat unexpected and therefore leave them confused, anxious, and subject to secondary stress because of their failure to understand that their reactions are typical. For instance, women returning to education may be afraid to admit that they are afraid of competing with younger students, that they are ashamed because of their age deviancy, or that they have lost confidence in their own abilities. They may believe that these emotions are a sign of weakness on their part and thus be doubly disturbed. By participating in a group composed of other adult women returning to education, they will have the opportunity to learn that these feelings are shared and that they are not abnormal.

If the program takes the form of a series of seminars, lectures, and workshops, then the support group is provided ready-made, so to speak. But the support group need not be formal, in the sense of meeting at a regularly scheduled time and place. Many adult centers, for example, provide facilities where adults can simply come in at any time, have a cup of coffee, and talk to other adults who happen to be there. Weiss emphasizes the value of informal discussions, as well as the value of more purposeful discussion among the participants. At each meeting of Seminars for the Separated, the participants had a chance to come early and stay late for an informal discussion. In addition, the final meeting was celebrated with a wine-and-cheese party. Such activities gave participants—many of whom had lost their previous social networks—a sense of belonging and of continuity. Indeed, many group members became anxious when the series ended and requested a continuation of the meetings. Recognizing that what they really wanted was continued access to the support group, the staff decided instead to schedule a reunion six weeks after the close of the series, and this plan was apparently reassuring. By the time of the reunion, most had found other social networks.

Not only emotional but also practical support may be required. For instance, a widow or widower with young children may have problems with childcare or housekeeping services. A counseling center planning a program to deal with these individuals might consider the feasibility of acting as a clearinghouse for these services. It might also encourage group members to brainstorm and share solutions to practical problems of this kind.

Support need not be a matter of face-to-face interaction. For instance, the Rhode Island project for home-bound adults used telephone counseling, available during the day and some evening hours, to give support to clients. Telephone hotlines have proved successful in a variety of emergency situations, when people in deep distress need immediate support; suicide prevention units are an example.

Certain kinds of support may not be appropriate. In the second sample interview in Chapter 4, the client spoke of a well-meaning friend, obviously trying to offer a kind of support, who introduced her to another widow, a dowdy older woman; the implied comparison was obviously resented by the client. Nor do all target populations benefit from support strategies. For instance, adults who have made up their minds to change careers may not have any need for either emotional or practical kinds of support for this decision. What they need, perhaps, is definite information on career options; for such people, the introduction of cognitive materials is the appropriate strategy.

The kinds of cognitive materials available to help people in transition situations are so varied as to defy a complete listing. They may take the form of lectures or consultations, written materials, film strips and other such visual aids, training sessions including role-playing activities, field trips. They may vary in content from accounts of the experiences of other people in similar situations through descriptions of various educational programs or occupations to discussions of how-to-do-it.

For instance, the Goddard Space Flight Center program for mid-career employees included a counseling component and also placed the participants in different departments within the organization to give them actual experience at different jobs. The Rhode Island project developed career-related materials to be mailed out to participants; established the telephone counseling service; and operated a centrally based career resource center for adults. Weiss's Seminars for the Separated comprised a series of lectures on such topics as the emotional impact of separation, issues likely to create conflict between separated spouses (property division, support, custody, visitation), and the problems of building a new life organization and a new identity. Programs of assertiveness training usually include lecture presentations on the distinctions between nonassertive, assertive, and aggressive behavior, coupled with role-playing and modeling. One program for career changers consisted of a series of classes led by people from different fields who discussed job opportunities in their field for people in middle-age, as well as counseling services to help people match their own goals and talents with opportunities in the job market. Another program that performs a similar function is the INQUIRY project, a computer-based program built on the Tiedeman/O'Hara decision-making model described in Chapter 4 (Farmer, 1976, p. 50).

Not all cognitive materials need to be so elaborate as these. For instance, a program might be developed for the general goal of preventing child abuse and neglect, with the specific objective of making people more aware of the problem. For this purpose, different placards or posters might be designed and displayed throughout a community, or contact might be made with local newspaper, radio, or TV offices.

Let's take the example of veterans returning to education. The specific cognitive materials to be used would depend on the specific objectives of the program. A program designed to make veterans feel more comfortable in the role of student might consist of lectures covering such topics as the emotional state of veterans returning to school; a program intended to help veterans develop proper study habits might consist of skills training activities; a program with the primary objective of enabling veterans to "understand the system" might have discussion groups led by "veteran veterans" who had found ways of solving various problems. If the program were directed primarily at veterans who were not quite sure what they wanted to do, the cognitive framework might include written materials on how to plan for the future.

The third type of strategy for helping people in stressful situations gain a sense of greater control over their lives is planning. In particular, fairly long-range planning can benefit those in transition states, because they are in the process of trying to achieve a new equilibrium and may feel doubtful about where they are going and how they should get there. For instance, many men returning to school have a definite objective in mind—such as training for a new career—but others may have decided to continue their education for general self-enrichment or with only vague notions of what they want. The planning process gives them a chance to consider, in a rational and systematic way, their goals and the best means of achieving those goals. Chapter 10 includes an activity on life planning. Although it is designed especially for people making career decisions, it can be adapted to other kinds of decisions and situations and will be helpful to the program designer in deciding just what planning strategies might be incorporated into the program.

Evaluating the Program

Although program evaluation is an essential aspect of any kind of intelligent program design, it is one of the most neglected. Reporting on an American Institutes for Research survey of 367 adult counseling programs, Harrison and Entine

(1976) point out that one-third of these programs attempted no evaluation whatsoever. But if a program is to be effective, the developer will need to know just where it has succeeded and where it has failed in order to revise it for future use.

Some kind of systematic evaluation should be planned from the beginning. Identifying specific objectives, and stating them in action terms, is a first step. One must have a definite goal in mind if one is to know whether that goal has been reached or not. Yet many programs are developed with only the vaguest of purposes, making evaluation almost impossible.

Two types of material are generally used in evaluation. The first type is subjective reports by participants of the program's successes or failures. Such material has obvious shortcomings: lack of insight on the part of the participants, a desire to be pleasant and positive, and other kinds of bias based on personal considerations. Nonetheless, such reactions are valuable—especially if they are collected as feedback in the course of the program so that it can be improved as it goes along. For instance, the staff of Seminars for the Separated monitored the project by phoning participants after each meeting to ask them how it had been useful to them and what could be done to make it more useful; several revisions were made as the series progressed on the basis of these comments (Weiss, 1976). In addition, the participants were asked to make formal evaluations at the final meeting of the series and, again, at the reunion meeting six weeks later. A follow-up evaluation is particularly useful in gauging long-term effects that may not be visible immediately after a program.

The second type of evaluative material is more objective, involving measurement of changes in the behavior of the participants. Sometimes such changes can be measured by means of pretests and posttests. For example, a program designed to train older people as counselor aides had as one of its specific objectives training them to listen and respond effectively. Records of their interactions with clients were collected before and after this training to provide a basis for measuring improvement as a result of training (Bestul, 1977). Because many adult counseling programs do not involve specific skills training, however, such objective comparisons are often difficult.

Evaluation and assessment data must be meaningful to the organization supporting the program. For instance, an industrial program that ties its effectiveness to increased employee productivity is more apt to maintain its vitality and support from top management. The Goddard Space Flight Center program is presently collecting data on the effectiveness of its Career Development Workshop Series as related to changes in supervisors' performance evaluation ratings for employees who attended the workshops. These evaluation data are augmented by participant self-report data, participant changes in constructs such as external/internal locus of control, career maturity, and attainment of specific workshop objectives such as decision-making skills.

The thoughtful program designer will plan from the beginning for such evaluation and will devise ways to take measurements at various points, with the goal of improving the program. Like everything else connected with program development, the evaluative aspect requires imagination coupled with a willingness to be systematic and rigorous.

For activities and skills related to this chapter, see Chapter 10.

PART TWO

Skills

6

Recognizing and Combating Age Bias

As was pointed out in Chapter 1, a good part of our thinking about adults is couched in the form of myths. Myths are unsubstantiated beliefs that influence our behavior. They may be true or false or partly true and partly false; the point is that we hold them to be true without having tested and proved their validity. The myths that we hold about adulthood affect our interactions with people.

The activities in this chapter are intended to help you become aware of your own age bias, to understand the various forms it may take and its implications for counseling, and to explore more fully the nature and consequences of such bias.

ACTIVITY A: Assessing Your Age Bias

First, let us take a few moments to identify and explore some of the myths that people commonly hold about adults. Respond in writing to the Age Norms Inquiry (ANI) on the following pages.

AGE NORMS INQUIRY

Part I: Fill in the age limits in the blanks below where you feel that they are appropriate.

All Other Things Being Equal, a Man:

1. Can have a first child from ____ years to ____ years old.
2. Is attractive from ____ years to ____ years old.
3. Can remarry from ____ years to ____ years old.
4. Can date from ____ years to ____ years old.
5. Should be self-supporting from ____ years to ____ years old.
6. Can change from a career as corporate executive to a career as teacher from ____ years to ____ years old.
7. Can have his own apartment from ____ years to ____ years old.
8. Can go to college from ____ years to ____ years old.
9. Should begin his career from ____ years to ____ years old.
10. Can change from a career as bus driver to a career as sociologist from ____ years to ____ years old.
11. Can retire from ____ years to ____ years old.
12. Can divorce a wife from ____ years to ____ years old.
13. Should hold his top job from ____ years to ____ years old.

14. Is an old man from ___ years to ___ years old.

15. Can change his career from ___ years to ___ years old.

16. Can have his last child from ___ years to ___ years old.

All Other Things Being Equal, a Woman:

1. Can change her career from ___ years to ___ years old.

2. Is an old woman from ___ years to ___ years old.

3. Should hold her top job from ___ years to ___ years old.

4. Can have her last child from ___ years to ___ years old.

5. Can divorce a husband from ___ years to ___ years old.

6. Can retire from ___ years to ___ years old.

7. Can change from a career as bus driver to a career as sociologist from ___ years to ___ years old.

8. Should begin her career from ___ years to ___ years old.

9. Can go to college from ___ years to ___ years old.

10. Can have her own apartment from ___ years to ___ years old.

11. Can change from a career as corporate executive to a career as teacher from ___ years to ___ years old.

12. Should be self-supporting from ___ years to ___ years old.

13. Can date from ___ years to ___ years old.

14. Can remarry from ___ years to ___ years old.

15. Is attractive from ___ years to ___ years old.

16. Can have a first child from ___ years to ___ years old.

Part II: Write in the five adjectives that best describe:

A Man in His

20s

1.

2.

3.

4.

5.

40s

1.

2.

3.

4.

5.

60s

1.

2.

3.

4.

5.

A Woman in Her

20s

1.

2.

3.

4.

5.

40s

1.

2.

3.

4.

5.

60s

1.

2.

3.
4.
5.

Adapted from "Gerontology Program Evaluation Instrument," by M. Seltzer, Miami University, Oxford, Ohio; and from "How 'Age Biased' Are College Counselors?" by L. Troll and N. Schlossberg, *Industrial Gerontology*, Summer 1971, pp. 14–20. Based on material from "Age Norms, Age Constraints, and Adult Socialization," by B. L. Neugarten, J. W. Moore, and J. C. Lowe, *American Journal of Sociology*, 1965, 70, 710–717. Reprinted by permission.

Now read the scoring directions and answer the questions that follow.

Scoring directions. There are no hard-and-fast scoring directions. The Age Norms Inquiry is simply a tool to help you begin thinking about some of the age-related biases you may hold. The decision as to what constitutes a biased response is, in a sense, arbitrary. In Part I, if you indicated any age limits at all, your responses could be regarded as biased. Ideally, a nonbiased response is one that indicates that the behavior in question has nothing to do with age. For instance, a comment of "no age limit" would qualify as nonbiased. Read through your responses to Part I and put a *B* next to those items where you think your response indicates some degree of bias. To help in determining whether or not your answer is biased, try substituting various ages in the item. Is age the crucial variable, or could the behavior or characteristic in question be considered appropriate to age ranges other than those you have indicated? Now answer the questions below.

1. In Part I, how many items did you mark with a *B*? ____
2. Did you have more *B*s for one sex than for the other? Specify: Men ____; Women ____.

3. Compare your responses to item 2 on the scale for men and item 15 on the scale for women; to item 4 on the scale for men and item 13 on the scale for women; and to item 9 on the scale for men and item 8 on the scale for women. Did you indicate a narrower age range for one sex than for the other? Specify: Men ____; Women ____.
4. Compare your responses to items 9 and 15 on the scale for men; compare your responses to items 4 and 16 on the scale for women. Did you indicate a narrower age range for "younger" behavior than for "older" behavior? Specify: Men ____; Women ____.
5. In Part II, which adjectives appear on the list for more than one of the sex/age groups? Specify:

6. Did you describe any sex/age group with more positive or favorable adjectives than you used for the others? Which one(s)?
7. Did you describe any sex/age group with more negative or unfavorable adjectives than you used for the others? Which one(s)?
8. Did you use different adjectives to describe men and women in the same age group? Were these adjectives more favorable for one sex than the other? Specify:

IMPLICATIONS FOR COUNSELING

In responding to the Age Norms Inquiry, and analyzing your responses to the above questions, you have had a chance to recognize and assess your own age bias. In some instances, you may have found yourself responding in a biased fashion. Such responses are probably the result of cultural conditioning and of your past learning experiences. Counselors go through the same socialization process as everyone else in our society and so are subject to the same kinds of bias.

To review briefly some of the material from Chapter 1, we find that age bias takes three main forms:

> *restrictiveness:* the belief that certain behaviors are appropriate at certain ages and inappropriate at others. People tend to be more restrictive toward younger adults than toward older adults. For instance, people may find it easier to accept a 45-year-old man's returning to school to train for a new career than to accept a 25-year-old man's failing to have decided on a career.
>
> *distortion:* lack of congruence between the characteristics that "outsiders" ascribe to an age group and the characteristics that the age group ascribes to itself. For instance, younger people often assume that retirement is a traumatic event for a man who has been actively involved in a career during his adult years, but research indicates that retirement, if it occurs at the expected time, is often a positive and satisfying experience.
>
> *negative attitudes:* unfavorable or hostile attitudes toward any age group: for example, the notion that all adolescents are "spoiled," that all people in the 40–50 age group are stodgy, or that all people over 65 are senile.

All these forms of age bias have far-reaching implications for counseling activities. Most obviously, *age restrictiveness* may prevent us from dealing fairly and effectively with clients. Most of the clients that counselors see are considering options and making decisions about their lives. Unless we as counselors recognize, examine, and attempt to overcome—or at least control—these biases about what behaviors are appropriate to what ages, we may limit the options of our clients. Ask yourself: Have I ever discouraged clients from pursuing certain activities because of their age? Have I failed to present all possible career options because I felt that a client is too old to pursue a certain career? Do I support the same career choice for a 50-year-old as I would for a 25-year-old?

Counselors may also be guilty of *age distortion* based on erroneous beliefs about the characteristics of a particular age group. Ask yourself: have I ever made assumptions about what clients are like simply on the basis of their age? It may be useful to review your responses to Part II of the Age Norms Inquiry to check on what kind of age stereotypes you hold. You may test your *negative attitudes* toward particular age groups by asking yourself: How often do I tend to take an immediate like or dislike to a client? What is the basis for this feeling; does it have anything to do with the client's age? Do I tend to feel more comfortable with certain age groups?

Those of us in counseling must take responsibility for examining our own age bias. Activities such as the ones in this chapter represent a good beginning for such an examination. Periodic reassessment is necessary, and it is suggested that counselors repeat these exercises from time to time.

EXPLORING AGE BIAS

Now that you are sensitized to the issues of age bias and its ramifications and have become aware of your own age bias, you may want to explore more fully how age bias works to influence one's attitudes and behavior toward people. Activity B is designed to be carried out in a group situation. Activities C and D can be performed either in a group or by the individual working alone.

ACTIVITY B: Admissions Committee Role Play

The following simulated situation should be read aloud to the group:

Karen Adams is applying for admission to dental school. She is 40 years old and has always wanted to be a dentist. She has decided to apply to dental school now that her children are grown and she no longer has the full-time responsibility of caring for them. Her undergraduate school records and Dental Board scores place her in the top 10% of all applicants. The admissions committee is meeting to consider her application. There are five members on the committee.

Now the leader should ask for volunteers to play the five following roles:

Member 1. You have been teaching in the dental school for 20 years and are opposed to changing the graduate school's unwritten policy of admitting no one over age 35.

Member 2. You are part of the administrative staff and are specifically responsible for soliciting alumni funds. Your concern in admitting Karen would be the unfavorable response of several financially supportive alumni.

Member 3. You are a teaching faculty member who thinks Karen should be admitted. You suggest that the committee consider her qualifications separately from her age.

Member 4. You are a member of the Counseling Center staff who serves on the admissions committee as a universitywide member appointed by the dean. You have done a lot of work with adults who are trying to enter new careers or changing careers. You are extremely supportive of the applicant and are able to discuss the situation from the individual point of view.

Member 5. You are a teaching faculty member. You are ambivalent about admitting Karen. On the one hand, you feel that admissions should be limited to younger applicants who can devote more years to the profession. On the other hand, you vividly remember the recent race discrimination case that was brought against the dental school because of an admissions decision, and you fear that the same thing may happen in this case if you deny entry to Karen.

The activity is as follows:

1. Have the "admissions committee" meet for 15 minutes to consider Karen Adams's application.
2. Have the larger group discuss
   a. what issues were raised in the case, and
   b. what part age bias played in the "admissions committee's" deliberations.

ACTIVITY C: *Imaginative Projection*

The following activity is designed to help you empathize with some of the feelings of people who are subject to discrimination because of their age.

1. Decide on the age you would *least* like to be.
2. Take 10 minutes to record in the space below some notes on what the world would be like for you if you were that age. What particular problems might you have? What particular advantages might you have? How would other people treat you?

3. If working in a group, you may want to share your notes with the other members and ask for their reactions.

ACTIVITY D: Incidents of Age Bias

Record in the space below two incidents of age bias which you have either participated in or witnessed. Briefly describe each of these incidents and identify the form of age bias (restrictiveness, distortion, or negativism) present in each situation. The following is an example:

Incident: You are watching the evening news with friends, and one item concerns an outbreak of violence at a local high school. One of your friends comments, "Young people don't seem to have anything better to do with their time than to destroy public property."

Form of Age Bias: This is an example of negative attitudes. Your friend has expressed an unfavorable attitude toward young people, generalizing from one small group to *all* the age group.

1. Incident:

   Form of Age Bias:

2. Incident:

   Form of Age Bias:

7

Understanding Adult Development

The purpose of this chapter is to give you a more thorough knowledge of adult development and, in particular, to familiarize you with five developmental themes that characterize the adult years and that you will find helpful as concepts to use in counseling adults. Chapter 2 discusses the five developmental themes that are reviewed here, describes the work of several representative theorists, outlines a number of possible assumptions often made about adulthood, and summarizes empirical evidence on the physical, intellectual, personality, and sex-role changes that take place after adolescence. The activities suggested here will aid you in understanding and applying these concepts.

TURNING POINTS AND ROLE CHANGES

In the common view, adulthood—in contrast to childhood and adolescence—represents stability and certainty. It is assumed that people in the 25–60 age group have made their important decisions and settled into a steady and secure pattern of living, untroubled by the doubts, conflicts, and upheavals that mark their earlier years. But this view is patently false.

Adulthood is a time of change. Some of these changes are: leaving school; getting a job; getting married; having children; making a residential move; changing jobs; being separated, divorced, or widowed; advancing up the career ladder; retiring. Some of the changes that occur in the lives of adults are the result of deliberate decisions: to get married, to quit work and go back to school, to move to a warmer climate. Some are in the hands of other people: the employer who fails to give a promotion, the daughter who decides to get married, the spouse who packs up and moves out. Still other changes are beyond human control: the death of a parent or a spouse, a major deterioration in one's own health.

Any of these life events may be regarded as a major transition or turning point in life. These transitions may go smoothly and without undue strain, or they may involve some degree of stress—positive as well as negative—that exacts a toll on the individual. Frequently, these turning points involve role changes—either role increments (whereby one adds to one's repertoire of roles, becoming, for instance, a spouse, a parent, a full-time employee, a supervisor) or role deficits (whereby one loses a previously held role, as in losing the role of spouse through widowhood or divorce or losing the role of employee or worker through retirement).

It should be emphasized that not all role increments are necessarily favorable to the individual's well-being and life satisfaction: becoming a parent, for instance, may impose a heavy strain leading to severe depression; getting a job promotion may entail giving up the kind of work that one enjoys for much more boring activities. Nor do all role deficits entail pain and trauma: many people may experience great relief and a new sense of freedom when divorce ends an unhappy marriage, when their youngest child leaves home, or when they retire from a job. In addition, not all the turning points of life involve role changes. For instance, one may make a residential move or change jobs with neither role increment nor role loss. But often such changes in life circumstances do demand a new set of interpersonal relationships and even a new definition of the self.

In addition to the kinds of role changes described above, there is some evidence that certain sex-role changes occur during the adult years. Thus, Neugarten and Gutmann (1964) suggest that, in the middle years, men shift from a mode of *active mastery,* whereby thought and action are directed outward and the environment is perceived as challenging, something to be manipulated in order to get what one wants, to a mode of *passive mastery,* whereby the focus is turned inward upon one's own thoughts and feelings and the environment is perceived as threatening and hostile. According to this line of thought, women move in the opposite direction, from passivity and dependence to more direct and active coping with the environment. Another way to look at this sex-role change is to say that men become more affiliative and nurturant as they grow older, whereas women become more assertive and aggressive.

The following activities—the first to be carried out individually, the second to be done in a group—are designed to give you a better understanding of these concepts.

ACTIVITY A: Identifying Major Turning Points

Look back over your own life and record in the space below the three events that you regard as the most important transitions or turning points. Indicate whether they also involved role changes and whether those changes were increments or deficits.

1.

2.

3.

1. If appropriate, each member of the group should interview another member of the same sex and then a member of the opposite sex, asking them about any sex-role changes that they have experienced in their own lives or observed in the lives of others. Do they find evidence of a greater shift toward affiliation in the lives of men and toward assertiveness in the lives of women?
2. The total group should discuss the concept of role increments and role deficits. List some role changes on the board and consider whether they represent gains or losses. What kinds of changes in behavior are associated with different role changes?

STRESS

As indicated above, not all turning points or role changes are traumatic. Some may be made so smoothly that the individual is hardly aware of them. Neugarten (1976) maintains that only those life events that are "off time" are seriously disturbing to most people. Nonetheless, even positive changes may entail a strain that takes its toll.

Holmes and Rahe (1967) define *stress* as "those life events which require adjustment on the part of the individual." Their Social Readjustment Rating Scale assigns numerical weights to different types of changes. The person who has a high total score at the end of a given year is more likely to experience physical or psychological illness than is a person with a low score—though ability to cope with stress may vary from one individual to another, depending both on innate capability and on prior learning. The following activity is designed to give you a clearer understanding of the concept of stress.

1. Complete the Social Readjustment Rating Scale by checking those life events that you have experienced over the past year. Add the mean values of each event checked to get your total score, and hand it in on a slip of paper to the group leader or coordinator. The coordinator will list all scores on the board so that you can determine where your score falls in the total range.
2. The total group should then discuss the concept of *positive* and *negative* stress. Do any of the life events listed—such as marriage, pregnancy, change to a different line of work, change in residence—entail both positive and negative aspects? Discuss.
3. Can you suggest any other life events that might be added to the list?
4. Were there any differences in the kinds of events listed by men and the kinds of events listed by women in the group? Discuss.

SOCIAL READJUSTMENT RATING SCALE

Rank	Life Event	Mean Value	Your Mean Value
1	Death of spouse	100	
2	Divorce	73	
3	Marital separation	65	
4	Jail term	63	
5	Death of close family member	63	
6	Personal injury or illness	53	
7	Marriage	50	
8	Fired at work	47	

Continued on next page.

SOCIAL READJUSTMENT RATING SCALE
(continued)

Rank	Life Event	Mean Value	Your Mean Value
9	Marital reconciliation	45	
10	Retirement	45	
11	Change in health of family member	44	
12	Pregnancy	40	
13	Sex difficulties	39	
14	Gain of new family member	39	
15	Business readjustment	39	
16	Change in financial state	38	
17	Death of close friend	37	
18	Change to different line of work	36	
19	Change in number of arguments with spouse	35	
20	Mortgage over $10,000	31	
21	Foreclosure of mortgage or loan	30	
22	Change in responsibilities at work	29	
23	Son or daughter leaves home	29	
24	Trouble with in-laws	29	
25	Outstanding personal achievement	28	
26	Spouse begins or stops work	26	
27	Begin or end school	26	
28	Change in living conditions	25	
29	Revision of personal habits	24	
30	Trouble with boss	23	
31	Change in work hours or conditions	20	

SOCIAL READJUSTMENT RATING SCALE
(continued)

Rank	Life Event	Mean Value	Your Mean Value
32	Change in residence	20	
33	Change in schools	20	
34	Change in recreation	19	
35	Change in church activities	19	
36	Change in social activities	18	
37	Mortgage or loan less than $10,000	17	
38	Change in sleeping habits	16	
39	Change in number of family get-togethers	15	
40	Change in eating habits	15	
41	Vacation	13	
42	Christmas	12	
43	Minor violations of the law	11	
			Total

From "The Social Readjustment Rating Scale," by Thomas H. Holmes and Richard H. Rahe, *Journal of Psychosomatic Research,* 1967, *2,* 213–218. Copyright 1967. Reprinted by permission.

STOCK-TAKING

As adults move through various transitions and role changes, they experience certain subjective events. One of the most consuming of these is stock-taking—reassessing themselves, their options, their potentialities. Often they must face the difficult realization that they have not lived up to earlier expectations. Even relatively successful people may feel disappointment and regret, recognizing that their achievements have been bought at the cost of denying and suppressing certain aspects of their own personalities. For instance, the self-made business executive may suffer from a sense of loss because he has never been very close to his children; the woman who has fulfilled her roles as wife and mother may regret that she has never had a chance to become a journalist or to travel extensively.

Levinson and his associates (1976) maintain that at the Mid-Life Transition, which they say occurs in the early 40s for men, the long-suppressed Dream—the youthful hopes and visions of what life can be like—reemerges and seeks expression. Men and women seek to develop the unfulfilled aspects of their personalities. This idea connects with the crossover in sex roles previously mentioned, as men become more affiliative and women more assertive.

Stock-taking is characteristic of the middle years but can occur at any point when one perceives that options are narrowing, that certain potentialities are going unrealized, that the desire for completeness is being thwarted. Typical of such reassessment is the pervasive feeling that "I can't do anything to change my life now. I'm trapped. It's all over." As one woman wistfully remarked, "There are no more surprises. I miss that."

People react differently to stock-taking. Some, driven by desperation, may make impulsive and ill-considered decisions in the hope of escaping from the "trap" of their lives. Others, overwhelmed by their feelings, may sink into apathy and despair, unable to reach any decision or make any move. Still others may make use of the reassessment as an opportunity for positive change and development. Counselors, recognizing this issue of adulthood, can help clients to make more accurate assessments and to direct the feelings that accompany stock-taking into more positive channels.

ACTIVITY D: Dream and Reality

Take a few minutes to think of middle-aged clients or friends of yours who have had personal dreams that they have been unable to fulfill.

1. Pick one person and, in the space below, record the elements of that person's dream.

2. Discuss with the group the discrepancy between this dream and the person's present situation, and describe the feelings involved.

At some point in life, most people experience a dramatic shift in time perspective when they begin to think in terms of life-left-to-live rather than time-since-birth (Neugarten, 1968). Some of the factors leading to this shift include "the sense of bodily decline," a "more vivid recognition of one's own mortality," and "the sense of aging" (Levinson et al., 1976, pp. 24–25). Death becomes more real, one feels a greater distance from the young, and one becomes more compassionate toward the aged. As was true with stock-taking, however, this shift in perspective is not necessarily linked with chronological age; it can be associated with any perceived narrowing of options.

ACTIVITY E: The Life Line

1. On the bottom of this page, draw a line to represent your life. This line may take any form or direction: squiggly, straight, circular, whatever. Now mark an *X* on the line to indicate where you are right now.
2. In groups of five, spend a few minutes discussing why you drew the line as you did and why you put the *X* where you did.
3. In the larger group, discuss the adult's sense of time as it relates to planning for the future.

LOCUS OF CONTROL

According to Julian Rotter (1966), an individual's locus of control determines the way that individual shapes his or her life. An internal locus of control implies a sense of power over one's own life: one's own decisions and actions are of central importance. An external locus of control implies a sense of powerlessness in the face of overwhelming forces: one is at the mercy of other people, of social constraints, of fate. Individuals with an external locus of control are passive, unwilling to make decisions because they feel that such decisions will have little to do with what happens to them. Lowenthal and her associates (1975) found that the sense of inner control was the most important factor in whether a person made a successful adaptation to a major life transition.

Feeling out of control and helpless is related to profound psychological distress, severe illness, even death. Feeling in control is related to successful planning for the future. A prime goal of the counselor, then, is to enable clients to assume control of their lives.

ACTIVITY F: Determining Locus of Control

1. Take a few minutes to respond to the Locus of Control Scale.
2. Score your answers according to the Scoring Instructions following the Scale. Did your score generally validate your feeling of being in control or lacking control of your own life?

LOCUS OF CONTROL SCALE

Below are 11 pairs of statements. For each pair, please select *one* statement that is closer to your opinion. In some cases, you may find that you believe both statements; in other cases, you may believe neither one. Even when you feel this way about a pair of statements, select the one statement that is more nearly true in your opinion.

Try to consider each pair of statements separately when making your choices: do not be influenced by your previous choices.

1. a. ___ Many of the unhappy things in people's lives are partly due to bad luck. b. ___ People's misfortunes result from the mistakes they make.

---

2. a. __ In the long run, people get the respect they deserve in this world.   b. __ Unfortunately, an individual's worth often passes unrecognized no matter how hard he tries.

3. a. __ Without the right breaks, one cannot be an effective leader.   b. __ Capable people who fail to become leaders have not taken advantage of their opportunities.

4. a. __ Becoming a success is a matter of hard work; luck has little or nothing to do with it.   b. __ Getting a good job depends mainly on being in the right place at the right time.

5. a. __ What happens to me is my own doing.   b. __ Sometimes I feel that I don't have enough control over the direction my life is taking.

6. a. __ When I make plans, I am almost certain that I can make them work.   b. __ It is not always wise to plan too far ahead, because many things turn out to be a matter of good or bad fortune anyhow.

7. a. __ In my case, getting what I want has little or nothing to do with luck.   b. __ Many times we might just as well decide what to do by flipping a coin.

8. a. __ Who gets to be boss often depends on who was lucky enough to be in the right place first.   b. __ Getting people to do the right thing depends upon ability; luck has little or nothing to do with it.

9. a. __ Most people don't realize the extent to which their lives are controlled by accidental happenings.   b. __ There is really no such thing as "luck."

10. a. __ In the long run, the bad things that happen to us are balanced by the good ones.   b. __ Most misfortunes are the result of lack of ability, ignorance, laziness, or all three.

11. a. __ Many times I feel that I have little influence over the things that happen to me.   b. __ It is impossible for me to believe that chance or luck plays an important role in my life.

Abbreviated form of scale from *The Pre-Retirement Years,* Vol. 4, Manpower R&D Monograph 15 (Washington: U.S. Department of Labor, 1975), 225–357. Order from Superintendent of Documents, U.S. Government Printing Office, Stock No. 029-00237, Catalog No. L 1.39/3:151V4, $4.85.

Continued on next page.

LOCUS OF CONTROL SCALE *(continued)*

Scoring Instructions

Assign the score either (1) or (2) to each of your answers, then add the total.

1.	a = E (1)	b = I (2)
2.	a = I (2)	b = E (1)
3.	a = E (1)	b = I (2)
4.	a = I (2)	b = E (1)
5.	a = I (2)	b = E (1)
6.	a = I (2)	b = E (1)
7.	a = I (2)	b = E (1)
8.	a = E (1)	b = I (2)
9.	a = E (1)	b = I (2)
10.	a = E (1)	b = I (2)
11.	a = E (1)	b = I (2)

Scores range from 11 to 22 in order of increasing control. Plot your score on the following continuum:

External Locus	Internal Locus
11	22

ACTIVITY G: *Summary of Developmental Themes*

List below three of the five developmental themes of adulthood described in Chapter 2 and in this chapter. Define each theme briefly. Finally, apply each theme to your own or to a client's life.

1.

2.

3.

8

Applying Knowledge of Adult Development

The last chapter reviewed five developmental themes of adulthood and provided activities designed to increase your understanding of those themes. In this chapter, that knowledge will be applied to three different groups of adults: (1) men experiencing a mid-life crisis, (2) adults facing retirement, and (3) women returning to school. First, these three groups are described in terms of the five developmental themes (drawing on information from Chapter 3 on the arenas in which adults operate), and some of the programs designed to meet the needs of each group are outlined. Finally, you are asked to carry out a similar analysis with a population of your choice.

MEN EXPERIENCING A MID-LIFE CRISIS

As was pointed out in Chapter 2, there is a good deal of talk these days about male mid-life crisis. It has been studied by a number of researchers (Brim, 1976) and has received considerable coverage in the popular press. Whether such a crisis is inevitable in the lives of all American men, and when it occurs, are subject to some dispute. Suffice

it to say that many men do seem to go through a period of crisis at some point during their middle years.

Let us assume that you as a counselor will be working with a group of such men. They can be analyzed as follows.

Turning Points and Role Changes

The Mid-Life Transition, which according to Levinson and his associates (1976) generally begins in the late 30s and early 40s, is a "boundary region between two periods of greater stability" (p. 24). A mid-life crisis can be a period of considerable turmoil, even to the man who has been relatively successful in life, as he senses a disparity between what he had hoped to accomplish and what he has actually accomplished so far: in one way or another, he will have fallen short of the mark he had earlier set for himself. Moreover, he may feel that he has nothing to look forward to but role deficits. He may think he has reached the peak of his career or is trapped in a dead-end job. The prospect of retirement at some point in the future brings no relief; he may be worried about having enough money to live comfortably. He is likely to feel that he has failed in his roles of husband and father—or at least not lived up to his earlier ideals—and that it is too late to redeem himself. He may feel a need for greater affiliation rather than for assertion and achievement, perhaps just as his wife is changing in the opposite direction.

Stress

Often the nonoccurrence of an expected or "normal" event can be as upsetting as an event that occurs off-time or an event that is in itself traumatic. Many men in mid-life may experience stress because they have failed to achieve what they earlier dreamed of achieving: for instance, a job promotion that does not come through when it should, accompanied by the realization that they have gone as far as they can in their career. In the arena of family life, too, men may have reached a nadir in the disenchantment process. The very fact that nothing is happening in their lives—let alone anything positive —constitutes a stress. In addition, of course, some of the events that do occur may be stressful: failing strength or health, marital separation, death of a parent.

Stock-Taking

Stock-taking in the middle years involves a comparison of the earlier dream with the present reality. As mentioned, even successful men may be disheartened by the disparity between the two. During mid-life, men reassess the goals that they have set for themselves earlier. The outcome of this assessment is a decision either to settle for what they have or to change, often in some fairly drastic way. In some cases, the change may be sudden and ill-considered, the product of panic and desperation; in other cases, the change may be positive and can lead to further development.

Shift in Time Perspective

The shift in time perspective may be the most crucial issue for middle-aged men. At this point in their lives, they are likely to get the feeling that time is running out for them. Their interior monologue goes something like this:

> Here I am, but where am I? What do I want out of the rest of my life? If I plan to make a change, I've got to do it now. If I'm ever going to become a lawyer, an ecologist, a gem collector, a teacher, I'd better do it now! If I'm going to learn to read Greek, visit the cathedrals of Europe, climb Everest, I've got to act now! If I want to achieve happiness in sex, friendship, marriage, I'd better grab for it now!

Intensifying the sense that they have only a limited time left is the sharp awareness of their own mortality, the personalization of death, underscored by an awareness that their strength and vigor are waning. Many of these men have adolescent children who are giving them problems, even if those problems add up to no more than the children's failing to live up to parental expectations. They are cut off from the younger generation, unable to communicate. This distancing leads to feelings of isolation and loneliness.

Locus of Control

To the outsider, it may look as though a middle-aged man is admirably in control of his life —and, to some extent, he is. For example, the 40–60 age group has been referred to as the "Command Generation," because the people in this group—or at least the middle-class men—often hold high positions and make major decisions that affect the lives of others. In the vocational arena, these men are the bosses; in the arena of family life, they also may seem to be the authority figures in the eyes of their wives and children. In their own eyes, however, they often lack control. They are carried on by the momentum of events, by the force of decisions made in the past which they may now regret. Part of the lack of internal control is the sense that time is running out, as just discussed. Nonetheless, as is the case with other groups of adults, the potential for shifting from an external to an internal locus of control does exist: successfully coping with immediate difficulties leads to an increase in one's sense of control.

Programs

As the notion of a male mid-life crisis has come to be more widely popularized, programs ranging from personal identity groups to career counseling have been designed. Many such programs have sprung up in industrial and business settings, a reflection of the deleterious effects that such crises may have on capacity to work. Related efforts are directed at humanizing work environments and at providing financial aid to men making mid-life career changes. Another trend is exemplified by establishment of the National Center for Educational Brokering (NCEB), designed to help both men and women locate, and gain admission to, appropriate educational programs. Specifically, the NCEB offers information services, assessment, referral, and client advocacy.

For information on educational brokering and adult counseling in general, contact:

National Center for Educational Brokering
1211 Connecticut Avenue N.W.
Washington, DC 20036

Nexus
American Association for Higher Education
#1 Dupont Circle
Washington, DC 20036

For information on other mid-career counseling programs, contact:

Career Development Center
National Aeronautics and Space Administration
Goddard Space Flight Center
Code 140
Greenbelt, MD 20771

Mid-Career Counseling and Information Program
State University of New York
Stony Brook, NY 11790

Career Counseling and Guidance Program
University of California
PO Box 808
Livermore, CA 94550

ADULTS FACING RETIREMENT

Mandatory retirement at about age 65 has become generally accepted in our society; in periods when the supply of manpower exceeds the demand and when the economy is otherwise troubled, many workers are urged or forced to retire even earlier. This situation, along with increases in the life span, mean that many men and women may expect to spend more of their later years out of the labor force. Often, these people are healthy, active, and alert; the prospect of enforced leisure is not a welcome one. Thus, programs to prepare people for the retirement years are being initiated.

Let us assume that you are working with a group of adults, mainly men but some women, ranging in age from 55 to 63. All of them have spent most of their adult lives working. The group may be analyzed as follows.

Turning Points and Role Changes

Retirement from the labor force is usually viewed as a major transition point, a "rite of passage" sometimes accorded the same kind of public ceremony as graduation from high school and college. But it represents a transition to a period of life that is often viewed with trepidation. Work is central in the lives of many people, particularly men. Through it, they define their identity. To retire is to suffer a role deficit. One loses the role of worker (employee, supervisor, boss, whatever) in the work arena and the role of breadwinner in the family arena.

Although many people will take up new roles (often less clear-cut than the roles they are losing), even those who opt for early retirement and look forward to having the leisure to pursue other interests and activities may feel some doubt about their ability to put together a new kind of life for themselves. Others, having fewer inner resources to sustain them, may anticipate a complete vacuum in their lives. To them, the retirement years represent a kind of limbo before the release of death.

Although most of the research on the preretirement period has been done on male subjects, evidence suggests that retirement may be more traumatic for women workers (particularly for the divorced and widowed) than for men, whose wives have been able to keep familial and extrafamilial social networks intact (Lowenthal, Berkman, & Associates, 1967).

Stress

To people who have worked most of their lives, retirement obviously represents a major change in lifestyle, affecting every other area of their existence, and thus constitutes a heavy stress. The question becomes: how will I spend my time? Both husbands and wives look forward to renewing the warmth and intimacy of the early years of marriage, but at the same time they recognize that too much togetherness may change the form of their interactions and make for tensions. Complicating the situation, many people recognize that they may have to endure extreme financial hardship; social security and pensions may simply not be enough to allow them to live up to their previous standard, especially with inflation. Thus, the stress of retirement may be intensified by fear of poverty.

Generally, effective planning for retirement reduces the stress involved. Moreover, close and satisfying interpersonal relations seem to serve as a buffer against stress at this period. For example, older persons who live in an area with a high concentration of their age peers (such as retirement communities) have been found to adjust better to retirement than those who are isolated; they have many more social contacts, are much more active, and get substantial emotional support (Rosow, 1967).

Stock-Taking

According to Erikson (1950), the last developmental crisis is that of ego integrity: looking back over one's life and finding that it has meaning. He believes that the failure to resolve this crisis results in despair. Some adults in the preretirement group may already be involved in this crisis.

Shift in Time Perspective

Time-until-death becomes the focal point when one has retired, and those in the preretirement group are gradually adopting this perspective. Many at this point will feel that they are living "on borrowed time" and that their options have run out.

Locus of Control

As with the other groups so far discussed, having an internal locus of control seems to be critical during this period. Thus, Lowenthal and her associates (1975) found that the sense of control was related to having a positive attitude toward the impending transition and to planning for it. Men were more likely than women to feel in control. About one-fifth of the men in the preretirement group were planning second careers, and most of these men seemed to have made realistic appraisals of their talents, options, and possible problems. In contrast, women in the preretirement group, whether discussing their own or their husband's retirement, seemed to have done little planning and to feel little sense of control. As one said, "I don't really think too much of the future. You just kind of live from day to day. You just sort of know that you're going to retire and that you'll be able to come up with something after you do" (Lowenthal & Pierce, 1975, p. 207).

Programs

Programs to meet the needs of preretirement adults are proliferating. A recent bulletin from Nexus contained the following list:

Administration on Aging
400 6th Street, SW
Washington, DC 20024

Commission for the Aging, Baltimore City
Waxter Center
861 Park Avenue
Baltimore, MD 21201

Pre-Retirement Planning
Drake University
Des Moines, IA 50311

Pre-Retirement Education
Montclair State College
Upper Montclair, NJ 07043

Pre-Retirement Planning
2019 Irwin Road
Durham, NC 27706

Coordinator of Pre-Retirement
Active Retirement Center
Pace University, Pace Plaza
New York, NY 10038

Pre-Retirement Studies
Institute of Gerontology
520 E. Liberty
Ann Arbor, MI 48109

Pre-Retirement Project
Ethel Percy Andrus Gerontology Center
University of Southern California
Los Angeles, CA 90007

WOMEN RETURNING TO SCHOOL

A recent trend in postsecondary enrollments has been an increase in "atypical" students—that is, students who differ from the "modal" undergraduate, the middle-class White student in the 18- to 22-year-old age group. Larger proportions of minority students, low-income students, and older students are now entering the nation's colleges and universities (or, in some cases, returning to high school to get diplomas or enrolling in technical and vocational schools). Among the older students are many women who have somewhat belatedly realized a need or desire for more education. Many of them got married or went to work immediately after high school graduation; others may have attended college and even received a bachelor's degree. But now they have decided to return to school for one or more of several reasons: to develop or upgrade their skills so that they can enter or reenter the labor force or get better jobs; to "catch up" in their field for the same purposes; or to enrich their lives.

Let us assume that you will be working as a counselor with a group of such women. They range in age from 26 to 48. Most are currently married, though some are separated or divorced, and a few are widowed. The following analysis can be made of these women.

Turning Points and Role Changes

Many women wanting or needing to return to school for further education have been socialized to achieve vicariously (Lipman-Blumen, 1972). That is, they are accustomed to defining their identities not through their own activities and accomplishments, but through those of the dominant people (mostly men) around them: first their fathers, later their husbands, still later their children (usually their sons). Now they are making a transition from the mode of vicarious achievement to the mode of direct achievement. As students, their own abilities are on the line; they will have to prove themselves. Further, their need for affiliation may be giving way to a need for assertion and achievement.

In returning to school, these women will have to make major adjustments. No longer will they be able to devote all their energies to child rearing and housekeeping activities. Some may have to call upon their husbands to share these tasks. Some may have to give up or cut back on their social and civic activities. A number of these women have recently experienced role changes involving deficits (loss of role of wife because of divorce or bereavement); all will be adding the new role of student to their repertoire. Thus, they will experience some degree of strain. Indeed, they may be going through mid-life crises as dramatic as those thought to be characteristic of men in their 30s and 40s.

Stress

As we have seen, a stress is any change that requires adaptation by the individual. In this case, the stress may be both positive and negative: positive because many of these women are probably looking forward to returning to school as an enjoyable experience that means greater freedom and that will ultimately benefit them; negative because returning to school involves strain on their time, energy, and emotions. For instance, one woman in this situation reported feeling guilty because she could not take every car pool or have coffee with her friends as often as she used to do; another was anxious that her inability to keep up with housework

would lead to marital discord. Moreover, most of these women are fearful about the prospect of mingling and competing with younger students: they suffer from a sense of being age-deviant.

Stock-Taking

The stock-taking in which these women engage is likely to take the form of questioning their own competence: do they have what it takes to keep up with academic work after being away from school so long? Most are probably unsure about how to study, and some may even doubt their own intelligence and competence, particularly since they will be measuring themselves against younger people.

In addition, many in the group may be asking themselves questions related to their life goals ("How do I want to spend the rest of my life?" "What is it I really want to do?") and to their own identity ("Who am I: wife, mother, student, person?" "What do I really want to be?"). Some of the comments made by adult women participating in a special orientation session at the University of Maryland reflect these concerns:

> I'm a stewardess and back at school because of a nagging feeling that there's more to life than flying.

> I'm here against my husband's and my parents' wishes, but I'm determined to prepare myself for a career.

> I need something to do now that the children are in school.

Shift in Time Perspective

For some women, the perception that time is running out is what has driven them to return to school. They tell themselves "If I don't do it now, I'll never get another chance." They are consumed by a sense of urgency, even desperation. For others, the issue of time is related to the number of options they have defined for their lives: embarking on the new venture of returning to school may give them a feeling of having unlimited time. Also related to the shift in time perspective is the sense of distance from the younger generation, contributing to the feeling of being age-deviant.

Locus of Control

Women generally have little sense of being in control of their own lives (Lowenthal et al., 1975). It can be hypothesized, however, that those women who deliberately choose to return to school will feel an increased degree of control. They have reached a decision and are implementing it. But this hypothesis may not hold true for those women who have returned to school because some unanticipated event, such as divorce or bereavement, is forcing them to enter the job market. To them, the return to school may be an unhappy necessity, brought about by events beyond their control.

Programs

Numerous programs have been established to meet the needs of adult women returning to school. Many of these programs take the form of women's centers located on the campuses of academic institutions, whereas others are independent agencies in the community. Their functions and activities range from consciousness raising to academic and career counseling. Many provide support services such as child care and job placement; some offer support groups for major transitions such as marital separation and widowhood; others offer assertiveness training and guidance in life planning. Continuing education programs for women (CEW) are designed especially for these women, including such features as flexible scheduling, credit for life experi-

ence, and short-term certificate programs (Astin, 1976).

The booklet *Continuing Education for Women: Current Developments,* by the Women's Bureau, Employment Standards Administration, U.S. Department of Labor (1974), provides some leads to these programs. It can be obtained by writing to:

Superintendent of Documents
U.S. Government Printing Office
Washington, DC 20402

In addition, a fairly complete list of programs is available in the publication *Women's Centers: Where Are They?* (Project on the Status and Education of Women, 1975). It can be obtained by writing to:

Project on the Status and Education of Women
Association of American Colleges
1818 R Street, NW
Washington, DC 20009

ACTIVITY A: Analyzing the Population

Focusing on the five developmental themes covered in this and in the previous chapter, you are to describe in detail a particular group of adults with whom you would like to work. Note that the groups covered in this chapter are rather large and general. You may want to pick a somewhat smaller and more specific population of adults: for example, men making mid-career changes, divorced women with young children, retired people in urban communities, young couples expecting their first child, men approaching the age at which their father died, middle-aged suburban housewives. Include the following steps in your analysis:

1. Decide on the population with whom you would like to, or expect to, work.
2. Using the completion sheet on the next pages, first describe the general characteristics of the group as completely as possible: possible range of ages, sex composition, social class, occupation, marital status.
3. Next, analyze the group in terms of each of the developmental issues. Make sure you apply specific concepts as mentioned in this chapter and in Chapters 2 and 3. If you are working in a group, split up into pairs at this stage. Each member of the pair should "interview" the other as a means of eliciting information on the developmental themes as they apply to the population chosen. Summarize the discussion on the form.
4. If you are working in a group, return to the larger group setting and discuss some of the populations chosen and the developmental issues considered.

FORM FOR ANALYZING THE POPULATION

1. Description of Group

2. Turning Points and Role Changes

3. Stress

4. Stock-Taking

6. Locus of Control

5. Shift in Time Perspective

9

Developing Counseling Skills

As was pointed out in Chapter 4, counselors of adults require special knowledge and skills that are different from those needed by counselors of children and adolescents. Specifically, they must have (1) a knowledge of adult development, and skill in applying that knowledge; (2) the ability to listen and respond effectively; and (3) a practical understanding of the decision-making process. The first of these three components was covered in Chapters 7 and 8, which included activities to help you apply various concepts in adult development to specific populations. In this chapter, the second and third components are covered, and activities related to them are outlined.

LISTENING AND RESPONDING EFFECTIVELY

Listening and responding skills are frequently lauded as the keystones of effective counseling. They are particularly important in dealing with adults, many of whom are apprehensive about seeking professional help and come to counselors with a deep need for understanding and empathy. They have a strong sense of identity, a sense of self, that

must be acknowledged. They have already had some experience in adjusting to stress, making transitions, putting aside old roles, and adopting new ones. They have probably demonstrated various kinds of competence and chalked up different achievements—even if only the achievement of having survived—and they want their competencies and accomplishments to be recognized. Finally, they need to have whatever feelings brought them to a counselor legitimized—to know that their hopes, anxieties, and uncertainties are not unique, that other adults have similar feelings. All of these needs demand sensitivity on the part of the counselor, who must build rapport and open the lines of communication, so that clients are enabled to explore themselves, develop understanding, and decide on action to be taken.

Perhaps a starting point to developing effective listening and responding skills is an awareness of what to avoid. As a counselor, you should try *not* to reinforce the client's feelings of worthlessness and age deviancy—the fear that the problem is not important, that he or she is too old to change, that adults should be able to work out their own problems without help.

For many clients, understanding and support may be all that is necessary. Others will need help in expanding options, gathering information, sorting out choices, and establishing new directions. If you have listened carefully and responded appropriately, you will be able to give them this help. If, on the other hand, you have not heard the "subtext," and if your responses indicate that you are harboring some myth or bias, or passing judgments, you cannot establish the necessary relation that will allow you and the client to unite in a joint effort to work out the problem.

ACTIVITY A: Vignettes of Adult Problems

The following activity is designed to give you some practice in dealing with the concerns that adults often experience. The following eight vignettes are drawn from real life. (A half-hour videotape of these eight cases is available from the Educational Technology Center, University of Maryland, College Park, Maryland 20742. Supply tape and $5.00 for handling and postage.) After reading each vignette (or watching it on the videotape), turn to the Vignette Response Form on page 114. In the first column, record what your initial response to this client would be. Leave the other columns blank for the time being; you will fill in the second and third columns later in this chapter.

#1: Separated Male. I'm really feeling distressed. My wife and I have been separated for about a year and a half now. She just got back from vacation with my son and informed me that she is moving, out of the state, up with her folks. I have no input into the decision, I feel helpless, angry as hell; she is taking my son away. Any relationship I will have with him will be commuting 8 hours to go into a strange city, get a motel room, and invite him to the room. I feel no naturalness in the future situation. All she wants from me is the money to support her, even if she doesn't have the same costs because she will be living with her folks. I feel powerless, angry. I don't know what to do about it.

#2: Female Returning to School. I have been thinking about going back to school. My family is raised, and I have three teenagers who are in college. My daughter has been urging me to go back and maybe take a course or so each semester. But my problem is I have no idea where to start, because it has been so long since I've been to school and I don't know what kind of a course to take. I don't know what I would like to do. Would there be something of my own interest I would like to pursue, or should I pursue something in the business area, or what? I just have no idea. Also I don't know whether I would be able to study, whether I would be able to do a lot of writing, I don't know whether—you know, with a family—whether I would be able to devote the time to doing it, so I just don't know how even to begin to find something.

#3: GED Program Participant. I think I am going to have to drop out of the training program. When I first signed up for it, I really wanted to get my GED, because I wanted to be a nurse. But since that time I have found it really hard to make it on the $2.20 an hour that I get in training. I now have been offered a job over at the Hot Shoppes that pays $3.25, and I could really use the money, plus I'm not too sure I'm going to be able to follow through with the nurses' training anyway, because I found that it is going to take a long time, and I won't be able to give up working in order to go full time. I think I really should take this job while I can get it because I'm not sure that there are going to be any jobs available once I get the GED. A lot of my friends who finished high school are working over there, you see, and if I can get the job now maybe I should take it. So you know, I came to talk to you about it and to ask you what you think I should do.

#4: Mid-Career Male. Well, I really don't—I really don't know where to begin, I don't know what I am going to say to you. I just got this feeling that I'm kind of just dead-end, you know? I got a job, it's all right, but there is no future. And I see younger men getting ahead of me. Here I have a

house, a mortgage, I don't have the freedom to move as they do, but yet I get passed over for promotions. I got a good job, but it is going nowhere; it's just absolutely becoming part of my life that I don't like. I come to work, I do my job, I go home—there's no challenge. It's just kind of humdrum, I've done it many times before. But if I saw someplace I could move, someplace I could go, someplace I could get ahead, do some of the things I really wanted to do when I started in this organization. That's what I want. I don't know whether you are the person to help me or not, but it's just getting to me. I don't know where to turn, I don't know what I can do with my life at this particular juncture. The kids are getting older, I'm becoming less necessary there; you look at this organization, I'm becoming less necessary here. It's not much fun working here anymore, not much fun working, work is not what it used to be. I think I've got a lot to offer; I just don't know where I can go with it. Do you understand what I am saying, can you help me? I've just got to do something, I've got to move, got to grow.

#5: *Male, Child-Care Concern.* The main thing that I've talked about with you is the issue having to do with my wife. When we knew that Jan was pregnant the question arose as to how we are to manage that, because both of us work, we have equivalent degrees, equivalent positions. I had proposed the idea that I stay home a day or two days a week and go part-time on my job. That created in me and in her some real difficulties. I say I proposed it. It came out of a feeling that I should entertain the idea and try to process it through, and it turned out —what I thought would be a good idea, something I would enjoy—it turned out to be a lot of losses for me. One of the losses I wasn't even aware of was the fact that I give up some notion of success, I would have to change my success standards. I just couldn't compete successfully on three days a week, I felt, or if my peers were up here I'd be down here; and interestingly also my wife—it was easier for my wife to give up than for her to allow her husband to give up. But I felt some guilt in not being able to do it because I felt some notion of "shouldness." Somehow it seemed unfair that I go out and get a lot of money, meet needs outside of the house and she wouldn't, and she has given—she's three days a week at work and two at home and she enjoys that. In a sense I would enjoy that, too, but the losses are too great.

#6: *Veteran.* I'm a veteran from the United States Air Force, disabled and now attending the University of Maryland. The transition from the military to the university was kind of straining because, first of all, I was a boss there, and I'm not a boss here; and the age difference between my classmates and me could create some problems—in some classes it is difficult because I try to discuss things with them. They have been going to school all their lives, and I have a large gap where I haven't been and sometimes this is unsettling. When I first started at this campus I was lost and I had a little map and I was going from place to place. I would ask other students where something was, and they would kind of look at me and say, "Well, now, it's over here—I'm not sure where it is," and some think I should be a student and some think I should be an instructor, and I think because they are not sure which, this gives them an uneasy feeling. If I'm a student, why am I a student at this age? And if I am an instructor I should know my way around the campus. My counselor and I have a pretty good rapport, we understand each other, but still he is upset I guess because of our age difference. I'm older than he is, and this causes him sometimes to feel uneasy. I need assistance for classes—classes to take the subject matter. All of these things I still need assistance and if I don't get assistance this— the university, the bureaucracy—will crush you, and I need help in attaining that.

#7: *Widow.* I think probably one of the most frustrating feelings I had at Gam's death and previous to it was being angry, not just—I was not the only one that felt this way, but he felt the same. We were at a period where he had retired, although it was for disability reasons. It was at the point where he could have anyway and we—our children were grown—and we planned to do a lot of traveling (of course) and just do the things we wanted to do. When Gam first became ill or when he first retired —I should go back a little bit to say that he developed this condition about five years previous and had responded well to chemotherapy until about

VIGNETTE RESPONSE FORM

Vignette	First Response	Communication Block	Effective Response
#1 Separated Male			
#2 Female Returning to School			
#3 GED Program Participant			
#4 Mid-Career Male			
#5 Male, Child-Care Concern			
#6 Veteran			
#7 Widow			
#8 Female Job Seeker			

the last two years. Then at the time when he felt he would retire, he went downhill just so rapidly, and it made him so angry he would strike out against the bed, pillow, the wall, or anything just in anger because of what had happened. And if he had been a person who had not taken care of his health or in any way it would have been different, but it was something you couldn't help. He was also hurt, I think, for me feeling he was leaving me with the burden and wondering, if I ever got in the same circumstances, who in the world would take care of me. As Gam's doctor said, I had really earned my nurse's cap because I gave him a lot of the doctoring and the needles and everything he needed at home. I think the hurt also was seeing suffering and not being able to help except to give a shot that would last two to three hours. It hurt to put him in the hospital when I did because I had a sort of breakdown, I guess just nervous, so they call it. It's not like a nervous breakdown but exhaustion where you are dealing with something that is consuming all your time and energy of emotions. So I think that I—I don't know why—I don't know that you can help this in any way, but to try to get over this feeling of anger. When you try to get away with other thoughts once in a while, you're suddenly hit like that and, well, it—that's enough of that.

#8: Female Job Seeker. I really appreciate your willingness to talk to me today about my frustrations about not being able to secure the type of job that I am prepared and had worked hard to acquire, and I thought possibly you might be able to help a bit. I just finished working on an advanced degree in education and, as you know, at the moment the market is kind of glutted for teachers. And I am also in a situation where I can't move from this area if there were teaching jobs available elsewhere because my husband has a good job within the city, and yet I'm still very upset by the fact that I'm not able to pursue the profession that I'm trained for. I'm very interested in working with young people. I've done it for a number of years, and I don't like the idea that I'm maybe getting outdated and losing contact with people in the job market. I also find that, if I'm not working, I'm feeling insecure in my ability to do a job. That frightens me a great deal, and I was hoping possibly that you

might suggest some other outlets for me today. Should I continue to attempt to find a job in a field where I just know the whole thing is hopeless? It's very frustrating, particularly when you spend a lot of time and money in order to stay in the profession that I have had experience in and that I'm trained in. It's not only frustrating for me as a professional, but it has also indirectly affected the relationship I have with my son and husband, in that sometimes I can't help resenting the fact that I can't have the same freedom that my husband has in seeking a job. We do have a small child, and I devote time to his interests as well as my own, so there is a joint frustration.

Communication Blocks

In learning to make effective responses, it is sometimes helpful to start by considering what constitutes an ineffective response. The following checklist (adapted from Gordon, 1970) identifies and gives examples of responses that tend to block further communication.

1. *Ordering, directing, commanding:* telling a person what to do or what not to do; using the imperative. ("Stop that!")
2. *Warning, admonishing, threatening:* predicting dire consequences if a particular course of action is followed. ("If you do that, you'll be sorry.")
3. *Exhorting, moralizing, preaching:* telling someone what he/she ought to do or ought not do. ("You ought to get your mind off your problems.")
4. *Advising, giving solutions, making suggestions:* telling someone how to solve a problem, giving advice, providing answers or solutions. ("I suggest that you apply to a college immediately.")
5. *Lecturing, teaching, giving logical arguments:* trying to influence someone with facts, counterarguments, or your own opinions. ("You know that unemployment has risen by 1.5% over the past year.")
6. *Judging, criticizing, disagreeing, blaming:* making a negative evaluation of someone.

("That's very childish of you.")

7. *Praising, agreeing:* making a positive evaluation of someone. ("I think that's very wise of you.")
8. *Name-calling, ridiculing, shaming:* making someone feel foolish. ("What a stupid thing to do!")
9. *Interpreting, analyzing, diagnosing:* telling someone what his/her motives or psychological problems are. ("You're acting out your hostility toward people.")
10. *Reassuring, sympathizing, consoling:* trying to make someone feel better by minimizing the problem. ("You shouldn't worry about it; everyone gets depressed from time to time.")
11. *Probing, questioning, interrogating:* trying to find reasons, motives, causes; looking for more information to help solve a problem. ("When did these periods of depression start?")
12. *Withdrawing, distracting, humoring, diverting:* trying to get someone's mind off a problem. ("Just forget about it.")
13. *Categorizing, age-stereotyping:* trying to fit the person into an age category. ("Middle-aged women should give first consideration to their families.")*

ACTIVITY B: Identifying Blocks to Communication

Now turn back to the Vignette Response Form and read over your first response to each of the eight vignettes. Do any of them fit into the categories listed as blocks to communication? Then respond to the following two items.

1. In the second column of the Vignette Response Form ("Communication Block"), write the number of the category of block that you used in each of your first responses; put an *X* in any case where your response is not an example of one of the blocks.

*From *Parent Effectiveness Training,* by T. Gordon. Copyright 1970. Reprinted by permission of David McKay Co., Inc.

2. If the activity is being carried out in a group, the group leader should ask the participants to share some of the responses for each of the vignettes, and the group should discuss them.

ACTIVITY C: Blocking Communication

In order to experience what it is like to try to communicate with someone who responds with a "block":

1. Members of the group should pair off.
2. One member of each pair should try to communicate a problem; the other should respond with one of the 13 blocks to communication.
3. The pair should switch roles and repeat step 2.
4. Return to the larger group and discuss your reactions to blocking responses.

Effective Responses

Now that we have looked at ineffective responses, let's consider some of the components of effective responses and note how they differ from blocking responses. As was pointed out in Chapter 4, Carkhuff and Berenson (1967) propose a counseling model that specifies three sequential goals, the first of which is to help the client reach self-understanding. To achieve this goal, the counselor's response must reflect the feelings and content of the client.

Consider the following exchange:

Client: My husband told me that I'm starting to think I'm better than he is since I started vocational training through the new careers program.
Counselor #1: While you want to improve yourself, it's really frustrating because it seems to be hurting your relationship with your husband.
Counselor #2: This new careers program—does it pay your way through school?
Counselor #3: Don't you think you're too old to go back to school?

Counselor #4: Why don't you go home, make up, and cook him an extra-special dinner tonight?

Which of the counselors made the most appropriate response, reflecting the client's feelings and content? *Counselor #1* seems to have made the most effective response. If you were the client, how would you react to the responses given by Counselors #2, #3, and #4? What would your next comment be?

As a counselor, how would you respond to the following client?

My wife just doesn't understand my wanting to change careers at my age.

Does your response reflect the content and affect that the client expressed?

The following responses, suggested by Eisenberg and Delaney (1977), provide some additional guidelines for formulating effective responses. They suggest that the use of these responses will "facilitate communication and stimulate a more in-depth intense level of thinking" (pp. 91–92).

Summarizing: I want to be sure I understand what you have told me. . . .

Interchangeable responses, especially those that are worded so as to reflect feelings and beliefs: I hear you saying that you are angry that your wife does not respect your privacy.

Clarification-requesting responses: Could you tell me more about these feelings of confusion you get when you are alone? Could you give me another example of a time when you got so angry you wanted to hit the other person involved?

Responses that are intended to clarify feelings, beliefs, values, and assumptions: Is that something you are proud of? How might you express your commitment to that point of view? Let's see if we can figure out the assumptions behind that point of view. Were you upset enough that you really wanted to disengage from the discussion?

"I" messages: I am curious as to how you dealt with that difficult situation. I am eager to know more about your thinking on this issue. I am wondering about how your parents reacted to this news. I am confused about what you are saying to me. Could you clarify what you are saying so that I can understand more fully?

Low-level inferences: I am sensing that you were really disappointed that your boyfriend did not call you. I have a hunch that it was very difficult for you to be assertive in this situation.

Combinations: I hear the anger you are feeling. I am sensing you were especially disappointed that your parents did not tell you sooner about their decision. I am wondering if you took their actions to mean they thought you weren't mature enough to understand the problem.

Self-Verbalization

We have just looked at some guidelines for formulating effective responses. But how do counselors get to this point? What do they think about before finally making a response to a client? In Chapter 4, we talked about the process of self-verbalization—the kind of interior monologue that everyone carries out before actually vocalizing, even though the process may take place in a split second and automatically. We probably do more self-verbalizing when we first meet someone, because at that point we are trying harder to understand, to say the right thing, to make a good impression.

Counselors must become aware of, and focus on, the self-verbalization process to formulate more effective responses. One way to do this is to make self-verbalization explicit and vocal.

Adapting the work of Meichenbaum (1973) and Ochiltree, Brekke, and Yager (1975), we have put together the following list of questions that counselors should ask themselves in listening to a client.

1. What is the client expressing verbally/nonverbally?
2. How do I really feel about what a person his/her age should do?
3. How would I feel if I were in his/her place?
4. What would I really like to say?
5. What's wrong with that response?
6. What will I say? What is the least biased or most effective response I can make?

By answering these questions, at first vocally (out loud), and then subvocally, you can begin to focus on the self-verbalization process that precedes your actual response.

Turn back to Vignette #1—the case of the separated male who is angry that his wife is contemplating moving with his son. The following self-verbalization is an example of what the counselor might go through before responding to the client's presentation of his problem:

1. What is he expressing verbally/nonverbally? He's really angry and scared that he won't be able to see his son.
2. How do I really feel about what a person in his situation should be doing?
   Here's where my bias comes in—I feel that all children should be with their mothers.
3. How would I feel if I were in his place?
   Impotent, frustrated, angry. (Are these the feelings he's really expressing or those that I would be experiencing? Check his nonverbal behavior.)
4. What would I really like to say?
   It might go something like this: "I can understand some of what you're saying, but I think it's more important for your son to be with his mother."
5. What's wrong with the above response?
   It is subtly biased; it focuses only on the tradi-

tional child/mother relationship rather than on the child/parent relationship. The issue is where the child would be most nurtured, not whether he's with his mother.
6. What will I say? What is the least biased, most effective response I can make?
   One response that might work is: "It sounds as though your anger is all-consuming at the moment." This response might open up communication and establish a basis for considering alternatives without imposing bias.

By making explicit the self-verbalization process, you can begin to see more clearly how you influence an interaction with a client. You will become more aware of your biases and better able to anticipate the effect that your responses will have on the client.

ACTIVITY D: Practicing Self-Verbalization Out Loud

The group should divide into teams of three: one to play the role of *counselor,* the second the role of *client,* and the third the role of *observer.* After one role-play is completed, the members of the team should switch roles, until each member has had the chance to play all three roles. The activity consists of the following steps:

1. The client should take a few minutes to think of a real concern of his/her own, or one that another adult might have. The client should then express that concern to the counselor.
2. The counselor should answer the six suggested questions for self-verbalization out loud, ending with what has been decided upon as the most effective response, which should then be addressed to the client.
3. The client should indicate out loud how the counselor's response made him/her feel and should also consider how he/she would have

felt if the counselor had given the response indicated in question 4 ("What would I really like to say?").

4. At the end of the exchange, the observer should take a few minutes to comment on the entire process.

Like any skill, self-verbalizing may be difficult for some people. The procedure may seem somewhat strained and artificial. Practice is the answer to this problem. The more the counselor practices using this self-check technique, the easier it will become.

Obviously, in a real-life situation the counselor cannot self-verbalize out loud. Ochiltree et al. (1975) and Meichenbaum (1973) suggest a three-step learning approach: (1) vocalizing the answers in a normal tone of voice; (2) whispering the answers; and (3) answering subvocally. They also suggest that, after answering the six questions, you should ask yourself, "Is there anything I can pat myself on the back for doing?" You may want to add this as a seventh question. These "pats on the back" might include such self-verbalizations as "I think I did a pretty good job on that one."

ACTIVITY E: Refining the Self-Verbalization Process

Once again, the group should divide into teams of three, with each member taking a turn at each of the three roles: counselor, client, and observer. This time, the following steps should be followed:

1. The client should take a few minutes to think of a real concern and then express that concern to the counselor.
2. The counselor should respond to the client's concern, and the interchange should continue (with further input from the client) until the counselor has had the chance to make five responses.
3. The observer should use the Rating Grid to comment on the effectiveness of each of these responses, based on the following three criteria:
   a. Did the response focus on the feelings and content that the client was expressing?
   b. Was the response free of bias, neither leading the interaction in a particular direction nor limiting options?
   c. Did the response enhance the interaction? Did the client continue to communicate?

RATING GRID FOR ACTIVITY E

(To be used by observer; please include relevant comments.)

	Criteria		
Counselor	a	b	c
1st Response			
2nd Response			

Continued on next page.

RATING GRID FOR ACTIVITY E *(continued)*

Counselor	Criteria		
	a	b	c
3rd Response			
4th Response			
5th Response			

ACTIVITY F: Making Appropriate Responses

Now that you have had some practice in self-verbalizing and in making appropriate responses, turn back to the Vignette Rating Form and fill in the third column for each of the eight cases ("Effective Response").

APPLYING THE DECISION-MAKING MODEL

A primary goal of the counseling process is to enable the client to gain a feeling of control over his/her own life. Research evidence indicates that many people are characterized by an external locus of control: they feel that their lives are manipulated by forces outside themselves. Those forces may consist of other people (spouse, children, employer), or they may be more general and impersonal (a tight job market). Whatever the precise situation, it is characterized by a feeling of helplessness. Often, this helplessness is illusory. People may be far more in control of their lives than they are aware of or care to acknowledge. To be in control, of course, implies a willingness to take responsibility for one's life, and some people may find this very difficult.

ACTIVITY G: "Have to" versus "Choose to"

This activity is designed to get you to examine the issue of control in your own life and to demonstrate that you may be more in control than you think.

1. Take a few minutes to think of three *have to's* (things that you feel you must do) and three *choose to's* (things that you feel you have some choice in doing) in your life. Record them in the space below:

I have to:	I choose to:
a.	a.
b.	b.
c.	c.

2. Now go back over the *have to's* and see if you can change any of them to *choose to's*. Aren't some of the activities that you feel you must do—for example, work at a particular job or go to school —really the result of earlier choices that you have made? Couldn't you *not* do them if you chose to (and were willing to take the consequences)?

The Two Stages of Decision Making

In Chapter 4, we introduced a decision-making model, proposed by Tiedeman and O'Hara (1963), that defined two main stages in making any decision: anticipation and implementation.

The first phase of the anticipation stage is *exploration,* which involves fantasizing; assessing interests, values, and skills; developing options and gathering information on them. As the anticipatory stage progresses, the individual evaluates various alternatives in terms of their possible or probable outcomes, rejects some, and gradually narrows the focus and makes a choice. This second phase is called *crystallization.*

The implementation stage starts with *induction,* when the individual enters the new system. Gradually the individual gains a sense of self in the new role and is accepted by others in the system. This last phase is called *integration.*

The adult who comes to a counselor for help may be either in the anticipation or in the implementation phase of the decision-making process. The counselor must first decide just where the client is.

ACTIVITY H: Anticipation or Implementation?

1. Go back to the vignettes at the beginning of this chapter (Activity A) and look again at #2 (the woman who is thinking about going back to school), #4 (the man who feels "boxed-in" at his present job), and #8 (the woman with an advanced degree who can't find a job in her field). Using the Decision-Making Worksheet, summarize the nature of each decision in the second column. In the third column, indicate where each of these three adults is in the decision-making process: at the anticipation or the implementation stage. (Mark an *A* or an *I* in the third column.)

2. If you are working in a group, the group leader should write on the board the consensus of the class as to the stage that each of these adults has reached; the group should then discuss why they made that classification.

3. Next, think of a career decision that you are facing right now. If you can't think of a personal career decision you must make, think of a decision that one of your clients or friends may be making. On the Decision-Making Worksheet, briefly describe that decision in the section labeled "your own example"; then indicate whether it falls in the anticipation or the implementation stage, by marking an *A* or an *I* in the third column. (You will be completing the rest of the Worksheet later in this chapter.)

Identifying where a person is in the decision-making process is a first step. The next step is to suggest strategies to help the person move along in the process. We are going to examine selected strategies that can be used at different points. Most of our examples are related to career decisions, but these

DECISION-MAKING WORKSHEET

Identification	Nature of Decision	Stage	Strategies	Alternatives
#2 Female Returning to School				
#4 Mid-Career Male				
#8 Female Job Seeker				
Your own example				

strategies can be applied to decisions in other areas as well. For those of you who want to learn more, we have included references to various books and commercial programs that deal with the strategies in greater depth.

Anticipation Strategies

At this stage, the individual should first be encouraged to explore as fully as possible. This involves both self-exploration (assessing one's own values, interests, and skills) and exploration of options. Crystallization—the narrowing down of options until one is selected—will come later. The particular strategies to be pursued at this point are as follows:

Fantasizing and dreaming. All too often, adults faced with decisions are constricted from the beginning in their thinking. For instance, many women and members of racial/ethnic minorities may feel that very few jobs are open to them and that, therefore, they ought to consider only a narrow range of careers. The counselor can do a great deal to encourage clients to open up their thinking, to give their dreams free rein, to expand their horizons. At this point, considerations of strict practicality should be put aside in favor of freewheeling fantasy. The following activity is one that you should test first on yourself; you may later use it in dealing with clients.

ACTIVITY I: The Ideal Job

1. Take a few minutes to envision the job that seems ideal to you. Think about it in detail: What would you be doing? Where would you be? Who would you be working with? After you have the picture clear in your own mind, describe your ideal job in the space below.

2. If you are working in a group, you might like to share your description of your ideal job with the other members.

Clarifying values. People sometimes need help in clarifying what is really important to them. In making career decisions, they need to be aware of their own priorities. As a beginning, they might ask themselves: what are my long-range life goals? to make a lot of money and live comfortably? to help other people in difficulty? to win recognition for achievement in a particular field? to make an important contribution to science or the arts? to be successful in business? Only after their own values are clarified can people decide whether a particular career offers opportunities to live up to those values and to fulfill their long-range goals.

ACTIVITY J: Specification of Life Goals

1. Take a few minutes to think about what you want most out of life—your long-range goals. Then record them in the space below:
   a.
   b.
   c.
2. If you are working in a group, you may want to share these goals with the other members. Such a discussion will also give you some insight into the kinds of goals that other people have.

Another way of clarifying values is to focus on use of time. One's daily activities are, to some extent, a mirror of one's values. An excellent reference on this point is *Values Clarification* (Simon, Howe, & Kirschenbaum, 1972). Often, the impetus for a career change is the desire to change one's allocation of time so that it more closely reflects one's priorities.

ACTIVITY K: Allocation of Time

1. In the space below is a "pie" representing the 24 hours of the day; the dotted lines divide this pie into four equal parts of six hours each. Using solid lines, divide the pie into sections, each representing the approximate amount of time you spend on the following activities:
   a. on the job
   b. household chores
   c. sleeping
   d. alone (reading, watching TV, other solitary activities)
   e. socializing with friends
   f. other categories

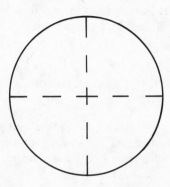

2. What conclusions might an observer draw about your values from looking at how you spend your time? Specify:

3. How does your actual division of time compare with what you said you valued in Activity J of this chapter? Specify:

4. Now slice the pie below to show how you would like to spend your time.

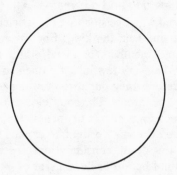

5. What would be different? Specify:

Assessing interests. Obviously, being interested in a particular job is a prime factor in career satisfaction. Few people are happy doing work that is distasteful or dull to them, though they may be willing to put up with their negative reactions for the sake of good pay or security. Our interests are the key to a wide range of other personal attributes, and measuring interests is a complicated business. Several interest inventories are available commercially that will help in such an assessment. Two of the most widely used are *The Self-Directed Search* (Holland, 1970) and the *Strong-Campbell Vocational Interest Blank* (Strong & Campbell, 1974). You may want to familiarize yourself with these instruments, though you should also be aware that both have been criticized for their sex bias (see, for example, Cole, 1972).

Identifying skills. In considering various careers, adults need to have a precise knowledge of their skills and abilities. Often, they may overlook some of their talents, and it is the counselor's task to help them arrive at a realistic appraisal. Some books that may be useful are: *Where Do I Go from Here with My Life?* (Crystal & Bolles, 1974), *Career Satisfaction and Success* (Haldane, 1974), and *System for Identifying Motivated Abilities* (Miller, 1971). The following activity represents a beginning.

ACTIVITY L: Identification of Skills

1. Take a few minutes to think of three of your own accomplishments—things that you have done or can do that you are proud of and that are important to you personally. Note that these accomplishments need not be limited to achievements in school or on the job; you may want to consider family life, interpersonal relations, leisure pursuits. Now describe these accomplishments in as much detail as possible.

a.

b.

c.

2. Now, for each of these three accomplishments, analyze the skills involved—the abilities that helped you to perform a specific task. Some examples of various types of skills are: verbal/persuasive, physical/athletic, numerical, social/interpersonal, leadership, artistic (writing, painting, performing), investigative. Record the skills required for each accomplishment.

a.

b.

c.

c.

3. Skills are usually transferable from one set of circumstances to another. Take a few minutes to
think about job settings where the skills you
listed above might be valuable. Record the job
settings in the space below.

a.

b.

Developing alternatives. The next step in the
anticipatory stage of decision making is to develop
alternatives, based on the self-knowledge generated
by previous strategies. At this point, the client
should be encouraged to brainstorm various
options.

*Gathering information about alternatives and
predicting outcomes.* At this point, the earlier
fantasizing and self-exploration give way to exploration of the environment (the world of work, in the
case of career decision) and a realistic assessment of
prospects. Clients may need help in locating sources
of information about various careers and learning
how to use them. Relevant information in making a
career choice might include projected manpower
needs, the education or training necessary (including the time and cost involved), financial and other
rewards of the career, geographical considerations
(the local or regional job market), and the implications that a given career has for one's lifestyle. Once
the information has been gathered, the following
simple form can be used to evaluate alternatives and
to predict possible outcomes:

Alternative	Advantages	Dis-advantages	Possible Outcome

Choosing an alternative. In actually making a particular choice, adults may find it helpful to have information regarding different styles of decision-making and risk-taking behavior. A useful discussion of this topic, as well as of developing alternatives and gathering information on alternatives, can be found in two books published by the College Entrance Examination Board: *Decisions and Outcomes* (Gelatt, Varenhorst, Carey, & Miller, 1973) and *How to Decide: A Guide for Women* (Scholz, Prince, & Miller, 1975).

Implementation Strategies

At this stage, the focus is on helping individuals to actualize their decisions and to deal with some of the problems that may arise when they have been inducted into the new system. We will talk about four such strategies.

Planning for action. The stipulation of long-term and short-term goals, with deadlines for reaching them, and the identification of forces that may help or hinder the accomplishment of these goals, are all a part of action planning. The following simple form could be used:

	Helping Forces	Hindering Forces
Long-Term Goals (Deadline)		
Short-Term Goals (Deadline)		

The individual should also consider how to turn some of the hindering forces into helping forces:

Helping Forces ⟵ Hindering Forces

Training in assertiveness. When they enter a system—such as a school or a new job—some adults will need help in expressing their ideas and presenting themselves persuasively. Women in particular, who have been socialized into passive and compliant behavior, will probably have difficulty in distinguishing assertive from aggressive behavior and in acting assertively. In many communities, programs in assertiveness training are now offered. In addition, *Stand Up, Speak Out, Talk Back!* (Alberti & Emmons, 1975) is a useful reference.

Developing job-finding skills. Interpreting classified advertisements, writing résumés, and being interviewed for possible jobs present problems for some adults. One useful exercise is to role-play anticipated interviews. Other useful hints for finding and landing jobs are given in *What Color Is Your Parachute?* (Bolles, 1972).

Joining support groups. Once they have been inducted into the new system, if they are having some problems adjusting to it, adults may benefit from participating in a group with other adults who share the same problems. Such groups can provide help and suggest alternative courses of action in solving problems. (This strategy is discussed more thoroughly in Chapter 10.)

Some Examples

The particular strategy (or strategies) suggested by the counselor will depend upon where a client is in the decision-making process. Take, for example, the following case:

> Nancy has a master's degree in chemistry and has been looking for a job for six months. She has already located a child-care center for her three small children, but she is somewhat concerned about her ability to combine working and fulfilling her role as a mother.

This woman is in the implementation stage. She has

decided what she wants to do and needs help in actualizing this decision. All of the implementation strategies suggested might be appropriate. For instance, she may need help in developing her job-finding skills, in learning how to change hindering into helping forces, and in expressing herself assertively. Once she has a job, she may find that joining a support group composed of other working mothers will not only provide her with needed emotional support but may also result in concrete suggestions for successfully combining her two roles.

Now take another example:

Bob has just been discharged from military service, where he received training in electronics. But he is not sure that he wants to continue in this field, which he found rather boring. He thinks that he would like to get a job working with people but isn't quite sure what fields to consider.

Bob is obviously in the anticipation stage. He may benefit from several of the strategies described, especially the early strategies that encourage fantasizing about possible options. He may also need help in defining his values. He may want to consider some of the skills he acquired in the army and compare them with the skill requirements of various fields.

ACTIVITY M: Selecting Strategies

1. Turn back to the Decision-Making Worksheet (p. 122) and consider again the cases of the three adults from the vignettes (#2, #4, and #8). You have already identified what stage they are at in the decision-making process. Now, in the third column, indicate possible strategies that you might recommend to them.
2. If you are working in a group, you may want to share the suggested strategies with other members and to talk about why these strategies might prove useful in each case.

3. Now look again at your own example on the Decision-Making Worksheet and record possible strategies.

ACTIVITY N: Developing Alternatives

The final column on the Decision-Making Worksheet is entitled "Alternatives." This step is crucial in any decision-making situation. An adult involved in making a decision should be encouraged to consider as many alternatives as possible before worrying about narrowing them down.

1. In the fourth column of the Decision-Making Worksheet, list three possible alternatives for each of the adults from the vignettes. Make sure that they are realistic enough to be implemented by the person.
2. If you are working in a group, you may want to share these suggested alternatives with the other members and discuss why you selected them.
3. Now look again at your own example and record three alternatives.

ACTIVITY O: Decision-Making Role-Play

This activity is designed to help you put together the information and skills you have developed in this chapter: listening and responding effectively, and applying the decision-making model.

The group should divide into teams of three: one to play the role of *counselor;* the second to play the role of *client;* and the third to play the role of *observer.* After one role-play is completed, the members of the team should switch roles until each person has had the chance to play all three roles.

1. The client should share or express a decision-making situation selected to be used in the role-play.

2. The counselor should formulate and give a response.
3. The observer should comment on the effectiveness of the response.
4. The client should share with the counselor and the observer the three alternatives written down for your own example.
5. Finally, the counselor and the observer should try to generate at least three more alternatives for the client's decision-making example.

Planning Programs

In addition to working directly with adults in a face-to-face interaction, the counselor must often take on the role of program planner, designing programs for groups of adults experiencing similar life situations. For instance, effective programs have been designed for widows and widowers, people making mid-career changes, people recently divorced or separated from their spouses, minority women who need to upgrade their skills to get better jobs, parents who abuse their children, and various other groups within the population that are large enough, and whose needs are significant enough, to profit from programs but who might not ordinarily seek counseling on an individual basis.

In this chapter, we will review briefly some of the material in Chapter 5. Then you will be given a chance to develop a program for your target population (selected in Chapter 8), based on four developmental components, and to gain some experience in life planning. In carrying out these activities, you will be drawing on knowledge and skills acquired in previous chapters, including your practical understanding of adult development and your knowledge of the decision-making process and of how to apply that knowledge in selecting strategies that might prove helpful to particular clients.

The first activity is designed to stimulate your thinking about program development.

ACTIVITY A: Turning Alternatives into Programs

In Chapter 9, you were presented with eight vignettes of people seeking counseling. For three of these vignettes—#2 (the woman who is thinking of going back to school), #4 (the man who feels "boxed-in" in his present job), and #8 (the woman with an advanced degree who can't find a job in her field)—you were asked to consider strategies that might be helpful and also to list three alternative courses of action for each of the three adults (see Decision-Making Worksheet, p. 122).

1. Select one of the alternatives for each client that seems to you capable of being developed into a program designed to reach other adults in a similar situation. Using the Program Planning Sheet, enter that alternative in the first column. Now, translate that alternative into a statement of a general program objective (see Chapter 5, p. 80); record that objective in the second column.
2. Now, translate that general goal into a statement of a specific program objective, phrased in action

PROGRAM PLANNING SHEET

Identification	Alternative	General and Specific Program Objectives	Program Strategies
#2 Female Returning to School			
#4 Mid-Career Male			
#8 Female Job Seeker			

terms (see Chapter 5, p. 80); and record this also in the second column. (Later on in this chapter, you will be asked to fill in the third column.)

SITUATIONS AND STRATEGIES

As we saw in Chapter 5, people may be classified into three groups, depending on the kind of stressful situation they may be experiencing: (1) people in *crisis,* who are encountering a sudden and severely upsetting situation of limited duration, which demands that they hastily summon all their resources; (2) people in a *transition state,* a period marked by a change from one life situation to another that frequently involves dealing with anxiety, tension, fatigue, and other forms of emotional upset, finding new sources of support, and achieving a new personal and relational equilibrium; (3) people in a *deficit situation,* in which a new and stable—but in some respect inadequate—life organization has been achieved (Weiss, 1976).

Different kinds of helping strategies are required in each of these types of stressful situations. Thus, people in crisis can benefit from support from others (professional or nonprofessional) in the form of understanding, sympathy, and a readiness to help as needed. People in a transition state can also benefit from both emotional and practical support, but they may also need a cognitive framework that will help them to understand their own sometimes bewildering emotions and to make rational and well-considered decisions as they seek a new stability. People in deficit situations may need a continuing, problem-focused support system (which includes some cognitive materials) to deal with the problems that recur because of shortcomings and inadequacies in their life organization.

To the two strategies proposed by Weiss—support and cognitive materials—we have added a third: planning. Here we will also deal with a fourth aspect of program development: leadership. As examples in choosing appropriate strategies, we will focus on two groups in (or facing) a transition state: men experiencing mid-life crises and adults facing retirement.

Support

The program planner should give consideration to structuring a group of people experiencing the same transition state. Both men in a mid-life crisis and adults facing retirement will be helped by learning that they are not alone in the feelings they are experiencing. The cognitive framework would then be presented in regularly scheduled meetings, where the group would also have the opportunity for informal interaction and the sharing of experiences. The program designer should also give consideration to other possibilities for supportive services that would help the group participants emotionally or practically. For example, adults facing retirement might be provided with facilities where they could meet informally when they wished, outside the regularly scheduled sessions.

Cognitive Framework

The group of participants should be provided with an understanding of their situation, which often occasions a welter of confused feelings that they may not understand. Through lectures, written materials, and other such devices, they can be provided with a cognitive framework that will bring some order to their confusions. For instance, men in a mid-life crisis could be helped to understand that some of their feelings of regret and sadness are occasioned by the reemergence of the dream of their younger years and by the discrepancy between their earlier aspirations and their actual achievement. Adults facing retirement could be helped to understand that part of their anxiety may be based on a perceived loss of role and of status.

Planning

The group should be provided with skills in planning and taking initiative to gain some control over their lives. Both groups used for illustration here could be helped by considering the many options that are left to them to develop their potentialities and to be useful members of society.

Leadership

The leadership role of the program designer can be viewed in terms of the three basic types of strategies outlined above.

First, the program designer must structure the support group by defining the target group, assessing the needs of that group, and making actual arrangements for the meeting of the group at a given time and place—whether for a workshop, a series of meetings, or whatever other format is chosen as appropriate.

Second, the program designer is responsible for preparing the cognitive framework for the meeting, workshop, or whatever. Chapters 2 and 3 provide the content of the material that could be used in structuring this framework. The form of the cognitive materials is a matter for discretion and imagination. Guest lecturers—either experts in the field or veterans of the situation—might be called upon; various activities and exercises designed to give training in needed skills might be used; published materials might be made available to the group.

Third, the program designer is responsible for helping group participants plan for the future. The Life Planning process (Activity C) can be used for this purpose. Though designed specifically for adults making career decisions, it can be adapted for use by adults in other transition states.

ACTIVITY B: Brainstorming Program Strategies

1. Turn back to the Program Planning Sheet and spend a few minutes brainstorming possible strategies to use in connection with each case.
2. If you are working in a group, the members should pair off and fill out the Program Strategy Worksheet. Use the same population, or target group, that you specified and analyzed in Activity A of Chapter 8. Try to keep your program manageable and realistic, given your particular setting and the resources available to you.
3. Report back to the entire group on the kinds of programs and strategies you have developed.

PROGRAM STRATEGY WORKSHEET

Support

Cognitive Framework

Planning

Leadership

FOCUS ON LIFE PLANNING

The following activity is suggested as a comprehensive program strategy, emphasizing planning, for adults who are contemplating a career change. Adaptations of the program could be designed to meet the needs of adults in other transition states.

ACTIVITY C: Life Planning

Many people feel that their choices and their futures are largely determined by the past and controlled by other people. By giving you a chance to develop some long-range plans, this activity enables you to gain a sense of control over your own life. The sequence of steps presented here (adapted from Shepard, 1974) is designed for adults who are making career decisions, but it can also be adapted to

other types of decisions. Each step can be worked on alone and then, if you are working in a group, shared with the other members. The first few steps are warm-up exercises, designed to start you thinking about yourself and your goals. Gradually, you will zero in on a specific decision.

I. Self-Description

1. Write down ten answers to the question "Who am I?"
   a.
   b.
   c.
   d.
   e.
   f.
   g.
   h.
   i.
   j.

You have your own way of thinking about yourself. Perhaps you think of yourself in terms of the roles you play or the activities you engage in. Perhaps you think of yourself in terms of attributes and traits, positive or negative. Most likely you think of yourself in some combination of these frameworks.

2. Now look back over the ten items in your self-description and rank-order them in terms of their importance to you. Did the sequence change from the original order in which you wrote them down?

3. Now look again at your list and decide:
   a. Which of the items are permanent and which are temporary?
   b. Which items are you proud of? That is, which would you like to take with you into the future? Specify:

c. Which items are you ashamed of? That is, which would you just as soon leave behind you in the past? Specify:

d. Are there other items you would like to add to your self-description? Specify:

II. Autobiographical Account

1. Imagine that you have lived a long life and are writing a brief autobiographical account for posterity. What would you want it to say?

2. If you are working in a group, discuss what you have written with the other members.

3. If you were writing the autobiographical sketch now, instead of at the end of your life, what would it say? What do you have left to accomplish? Specify:

III. Ideal Year

1. Imagine that you were given unlimited resources to spend a year any way you wanted. What would that year be like? What would you do? Specify:

2. If you are working in a group, discuss what you have written with the other members.

IV. Ideal Job

1. In Activity I of Chapter 9, you described your ideal job. Look back at that description to refresh your memory. Then consider your present job. What are the differences between your real and your ideal job? Specify:

2. Now look again at your autobiographical account in Part II of this activity. That account indicated various accomplishments that you would like to be able to look back on at the end of your life. Is your ideal job consistent with the life goals implied in that account? Specify:

V. Career Inventory

1. Consider your present job and answer the following questions about it:

   a. What is there about the job that really excites me? When do I feel really alive?

   b. What do I do particularly well in my present job?

   c. What do I do poorly?

   d. What do I need to learn to do a better job?

   e. What skills do I use?

   f. What skills do I have that I am not using?

2. Begin to write a program for your own career development, keeping in mind your present and ideal job, your resources and abilities, and your life goals. Start by identifying a specific career objective: what is it you would like to be moving toward?

3. Now brainstorm some strategies that you might use to move toward that specific career objective. (If you are working in a group, you may want to pair off with another member to discuss possible strategies.) Select a specific strategy.

4. Consider what resources you now have available to you for carrying out that strategy. Examples are training, experience, time, family support, and financial resources.

VI. Action Plan

1. Consider and record the first three steps that you would take to implement your career strategy. Indicate the deadlines.

Steps   *Deadline*

a.

b.

c.

2. Now list some of the helping forces that might assist you in reaching your goal and some of the hindering forces that might prevent or delay your reaching it. Helping forces might be some of the resources you listed in item V-4. Hindering forces could be anything that might prevent you

from reaching your goal, such as lack of financial resources or opposition from your family.

Helping Forces   *Hindering Forces*

3. Weigh each of these forces. Which do you have control over? Can you reduce any of the hindering forces, or change them into helping forces? Discuss with the group.

COMPREHENSIVE PROGRAM DEVELOPMENT

The activities in this chapter have focused primarily on one aspect of program planning: selecting and designing appropriate strategies. However, as discussed in Chapter 5, in order to develop effective programs, all four of the following components must be included: (1) defining the target group, (2) identifying specific objectives, (3) designing and selecting strategies, and (4) evaluating the program. The following questions and pointers provide a framework for considering all four components of program planning.

ACTIVITY D: Steps toward Effective Program Development

Using the same target group as in Activity B, work through the following steps in planning an effective program for that group.

1. What are the needs of the individuals in your group? How do you know? How can you find out?
2. Where is your group in terms of meeting these needs?
3. Select one area of need and specify one goal related to this need that you want to work on. Be specific.
4. Brainstorm about your goal and different ways to approach it.
5. Analyze the forces that might help and those that might hinder the implementation of your goal.

Helping Forces   *Hindering Forces*

6. Brainstorm ways to capitalize on the helping forces and to minimize the hindrances.
7. As a means of making your goal more manageable, specify the first small step you will take.
8. What role will you as a leader play in implementing your goal?
9. Indicate a timetable for completion of your goal; specify when the first step will be completed.
10. Identify indicators of success: how will you know if your goal has been successfully achieved?*

*Reprinted from Robert S. Fox, Ronald Lippitt, and Eva Schindler-Rainman, *The Humanized Future: Some New Images*. La Jolla, Calif.: University Associates, 1973. Used with permission.

A Final Word

This book is based on the view that adults are capable of developing—of remaining open to experience and of integrating that experience to reach higher levels of complexity. The adults whom counselors are likely to see are seeking help for any one of a variety of reasons: because they are having difficulty deciding on a career, because they are having marital problems, because they are troubled by feelings of inadequacy or frustration or failure in their lives. Whatever their reasons, they are likely to be people whose lives have become uncertain and chaotic and who are seeking a new kind of equilibrium. Counselors can help assure that the change is more than just change—that it entails positive development.

But counselors will be less than useless—may indeed be highly destructive—if they themselves take the view that adulthood is a static period, that there is only one proper way to be mature, and that all deviations from that norm are to be discouraged —if, in short, they are age biased. Although age bias in various forms—restrictiveness, distortion, negative attitudes—is widespread and deep-rooted, and though counselors are as subject to it as any other human beings who have grown up in this society, it is our belief that they can become aware of their agism and by conscious effort overcome it, or at least control it as they deal with clients.

It is also our belief that too many people today feel out of control of their own lives, regarding themselves as pawns who are under pressure from inescapable forces that they cannot influence. The pervasiveness of this sense of helplessness can hardly be overstated: the young person who must make a career choice or take a job before he or she is ready to do so, the young parent who feels weighted down by the demanding daily routine of caring for an infant and keeping house, the worker caught in a 9-to-5 prison of meaningless and boring tasks, the middle-aged housewife who sees all chances of liberation and achievement slipping inexorably away from her, the successful businessperson who at age 50 suddenly realizes that he/she ignored important aspects of life and that time is running out—all these people suffer from the same feeling of being "locked in." Nor can the insidiousness of this sense of helplessness, and the passivity it breeds, be ignored.

To believe that one is powerless, no more than a cog in a machine, can be used to deny or refuse responsibility for and control over one's own life. Thus, we have emphasized the centrality of decision making. At the same time, we have tried to demonstrate the importance of encouraging clients to expand their thinking, to fantasize about possibilities, to open themselves to their own potentialities. The two functions—enabling clients to take responsibility for their lives and helping them to liberate their thinking—are interrelated. Freedom carries with it the obligation of responsibility; but responsibility carries with it the promise of freedom.

It may be argued that this view is overly optimistic—even simple-mindedly cheerful—in light of the realities of today's world. What good does it do for a counselor to give support to a 35-year-old bus driver who is thinking of becoming a sociologist if economic conditions are such that he is lucky to have a job driving a bus? Is it appropriate to encourage a 50-year-old woman to go back to school for a doctorate when most graduate or professional schools refuse to consider applicants over the age of 35? Where is the propriety in helping people to expand their options if the world is going to shut doors in their faces? Does not such action require a combination of ability and energy beyond what most people possess?

Obviously, there are some conditions that counselors cannot change in their role as counselors or as program developers. But there is a third type of intervention, touched on in previous chapters, open to the counselor, and that is social action to change basic conditions. The action can be multi-pronged: it can include political caucusing, publicizing through the mass media, appealing to particular institutions or businesses, advocating on behalf of clients, or other methods of pressure or persuasion. We have emphasized throughout this book the principle that counselors not impose their own values on clients, that they refrain from thinking in terms of "should" or "ought." But it is entirely appropriate that counselors act on their own values in the larger arena of society, that they work in whatever way they can to bring about needed change. Indeed, it may be not only appropriate but morally imperative that they do so.

References

Aaronson, B. Personality stereotypes of aging. *Journal of Gerontology,* 1966, *21,* 458–462.

Ahammer, I., & Baltes, P. Objective versus perceived age differences in personality: How do adolescents, adults, and older people view themselves and each other? *Journal of Gerontology,* 1972, *27,* 46–51.

Alberti, R. E., & Emmons, M. J. *Stand up, speak out, talk back!* New York: Simon & Schuster, 1975.

American Institutes for Research. *Developing comprehensive career guidance programs.* Palo Alto, Calif.: AIR, 1975.

American Personnel and Guidance Association. Adult education is booming field. *Guidepost,* 11 February 1974, p. 2.

Astin, H. S. (Ed.). *Some action of her own: The adult woman and higher education.* Lexington, Mass.: D.C. Heath, 1976.

Atchley, R. *The sociology of retirement.* Cambridge, Mass.: Schenkman, 1975.

Becker, H. S., & Strauss, A. L. Careers, personality, and adult socialization. *American Journal of Sociology,* 1956, *62,* 253–263.

Beeson, D., & Lowenthal, M. F. Perceived stress across life course. In M. F. Lowenthal, M. Thurnher, D. Chiriboga, & Associates, *Four stages of life: A comparative study of women and men facing transitions.* San Francisco: Jossey-Bass, 1975.

Belbin, E., & Belbin, R. M. New careers in middle age. In B. L. Neugarten (Ed.), *Middle age and aging.* Chicago: University of Chicago Press, 1968.

Bergmann, B. *Statement on equal pension benefits for men and women.* Washington: TIAA/CREF Committee, American Association of University Professors, 1974.

Bernard, J. *The future of marriage.* New York: World, 1972.

Bestul, M. *An evaluation of a program to train older people as counselor aides.* Unpublished master's thesis, University of Maryland, 1977.

Bingham, W. *Change of occupations as a function of the regency of occupational self-concepts.* Ann Arbor, Mich.: University Microfilms, 1966.

Blenkner, M. Social work and family relationships with some thoughts on filial maturity. In E. Shanas & G. F. Streib (Eds.), *Social structure and the family: Generational relations.* Englewood Cliffs, N.J.: Prentice-Hall, 1965.

Blood, R. B., Jr., & Wolfe, D. M. *Husbands and wives: The dynamics of married living.* New York: Free Press, 1960.

Bocknek, G. A developmental approach to counseling adults. *Counseling Psychologist,* 1976, *6*(1), 37–40.

Bohannon, P. Dyad dominance and household maintenance. In F. L. K. Hsu (Ed.), *Kinship and culture.* Chicago: Aldine, 1971.

Bolles, R. *What color is your parachute? A practical manual for job hunters and career changers.* Berkeley, Calif.: Ten Speed Press, 1972.

Bortner, R. W., & Hultsch, D. F. Patterns of subjective

deprivation in adulthood. *Developmental Psychology*, 1974, *10*, 534-545.

Brim, O. G., Jr. Theories of the male mid-life crisis. *Counseling Psychologist*, 1976, *6*(1), 2-9.

Brim, O. G., Jr. Theories of the male mid-life crisis. In N. K. Schlossberg & A. D. Entine (Eds.), *Counseling adults.* Monterey, Calif.: Brooks/Cole, 1977.

Butler, R. Age-ism: Another form of bigotry. *Gerontologist,* 1969, *9*, 243-246.

Carkhuff, R., & Berenson, B. *Beyond counseling and therapy.* New York: Holt, Rinehart & Winston, 1967.

Cattell, R. B. Theory of fluid and crystallized intelligence: A critical experiment. *Journal of Educational Psychology,* 1963, *54*, 1-22.

Clausen, J. The life course of individuals. In M. W. Riley, M. Johnson, & A. Foner (Eds.), *Aging and society: Vol. 3. A sociology of age stratification.* New York: Russell Sage Foundation, 1972.

Cole, N. S. *On measuring the vocational interests of women* (ACT Research Report No. 49). Iowa City: American College Testing Program, 1972.

Colligan, D. That helpless feeling: The dangers of stress. *New York,* 14 July 1975, pp. 28-32.

Crites, J. *Vocational psychology.* New York: McGraw-Hill, 1969.

Crites, J. A comprehensive model of career development in early adulthood. *Journal of Vocational Behavior,* 1976, *6*, 105-118.

Crystal, J., & Bolles, R. N. *Where do I go from here with my life?* New York: Seabury, 1974.

Deutscher, I. The quality of postparental life: Definitions of the situation. *Journal of Marriage and the Family,* 1964, *26*, 52-59.

Eisenberg, S., & Delaney, D. J. *The counseling process.* Chicago: Rand McNally, 1977.

Epstein, L. A., & Murray, J. H. Employment and retirement. In B. L. Neugarten (Ed.), *Middle age and aging.* Chicago: University of Chicago Press, 1968.

Erikson, E. *Childhood and society.* New York: W. W. Norton, 1950.

Farmer, H. INQUIRY project: Computer-assisted counseling centers for adults. *Counseling Psychologist,* 1976, *6*(1), 50-54.

Feldman, H. *Development of the husband-wife relationship: A research report.* Ithaca, N.Y.: Cornell University Press, 1964.

Fox, R., Lippitt, R., & Schindler-Rainman, E. *The humanized future: Images of potentiality.* La Jolla, Calif.: University Associates, 1975.

Fozard, J. L., Nuttal, R. L., & Waugh, N. C. Age-related differences in mental performance. *Aging and Human Development,* 1972, *3*, 19-43.

Gelatt, H. B., Varenhorst, B., Carey, R., & Miller, G. P. *Decisions and outcomes.* New York: College Entrance Examination Board, 1973.

Goffman, E. *Behavior in public places: Notes on the social organization of gatherings.* Glencoe, Ill.: Free Press, 1963.

Gordon, T. *Parent effectiveness training.* New York: Wyden, 1970.

Gould, R. The phases of adult life: A study in developmental psychology. *American Journal of Psychiatry,* 1972, *129*, 521-531.

Gruen, W. Adult personality: An empirical study of Erikson's theory of ego development. In B. L. Neugarten & Associates, *Personality in middle and late life.* New York: Atherton, 1964.

Gutmann, D. Female ego styles and generational conflict. In J. Bardwick, E. Douvan, M. Horner, & D. Gutmann, *Feminine personality and conflict.* Monterey, Calif.: Brooks/Cole, 1970.

Haldane, B. *Career satisfaction and success.* New York: American Management Association, 1974.

Harrison, L. R., & Entine, A. D. Existing programs and emerging strategies. *Counseling Psychologist,* 1976, *6*(1), 45-49.

Havighurst, R. *Human development and education.* New York: Longman, 1953.

Hiestand, D. *Changing careers after 35.* New York: Columbia University Press, 1971.

Hill, R., Foote, N., Aldous, J., Carlson, R., & Macdonald, R. *Family development in three generations.* Cambridge, Mass.: Schenkman, 1970.

Holland, J. L. *The self-directed search.* Palo Alto, Calif.: Consulting Psychologists Press, 1970.

Holland, J. L. *Making vocational choices: A theory of careers.* Englewood Cliffs, N.J.: Prentice-Hall, 1973.

Holmes, T. H., & Rahe, R. H. The social readjustment rating scale. *Journal of Psychosomatic Research,* 1967, *2*, 213-218.

Horner, M. S. Femininity and successful achievement: A basic inconsistency. In J. Bardwick, E. Douvan, M. Horner, and D. Gutmann, *Feminine personality and conflict.* Monterey, Calif.: Brooks/Cole, 1970.

Hurlock, E. B. *Developmental psychology* (3rd ed.). New York: McGraw-Hill, 1968.

Kahana, B. Old age seen negatively by old as well as young. *Geriatric Focus,* 1970, *9,* 10.

Kastenbaum, R., Derbin, V., Sabatini, P., & Artt, S. The ages of me: Toward personal and interpersonal definitions of functional aging. *Aging and Human Development,* 1972, *3,* 197–211.

Kerckhoff, A. C., & Bean, F. D. Social status and interpersonal patterns among married couples. *Social Forces,* 1970, *49,* 264–271.

Knox, A. B. *Adult development and learning.* San Francisco: Jossey-Bass, 1977.

Kohlberg, L. Continuities in childhood and adult moral development revisited. In P. B. Baltes & K. W. Schaie (Eds.), *Life-span developmental psychology: Personality and socialization.* New York: Academic Press, 1973.

LeMasters, E. E. Parenthood as crisis. *Marriage and Family,* 1957, *19,* 352–355.

Levinson, D. J., Darrow, C. M., Klein, E. B., Levinson, M. H., & McKee, B. Periods in the adult development of men: Ages 18 to 45. *Counseling Psychologist,* 1976, *6*(1), 21–25.

Levinson, D. J., Darrow, C. M., Klein, E. B., Levinson, M. H., & McKee, B. Periods in the adult development of men: Ages 18 to 45. In N. K. Schlossberg & A. D. Entine (Eds.), *Counseling adults.* Monterey, Calif.: Brooks/Cole, 1977.

Lipman-Blumen, J. How ideology shapes women's lives. *Scientific American,* 1972, *226*(1), 34–42.

Loevinger, J. *Ego development: Conceptions and theories.* San Francisco: Jossey-Bass, 1976.

Lopata, H. Z. *Occupation: Housewife.* London: Oxford University Press, 1971.

Lopata, H. Z. *Widowhood in an American city.* Cambridge, Mass.: Schenkman, 1973.

Lowenthal, M. F. Some potentialities of a life-cycle approach to the study of retirement. In F. M. Carp (Ed.), *Retirement.* New York: Behavioral Publications, 1972.

Lowenthal, M. F., Berkman, P. L., & Associates. *Aging and mental disorder in San Francisco: A social psychiatric study.* San Francisco: Jossey-Bass, 1967.

Lowenthal, M. F., & Chiriboga, D. Responses to stress. In M. F. Lowenthal, M. Thurnher, D. Chiriboga, & Associates, *Four stages of life: A comparative study of women and men facing transitions.* San Francisco: Jossey-Bass, 1975.

Lowenthal, M. F., & Haven, C. Interaction and adaptation: Intimacy as a critical variable. *American Sociological Review,* 1968, *33,* 20–30.

Lowenthal, M. F., & Pierce, R. The pretransitional stance. In M. F. Lowenthal, M. Thurnher, D. Chiriboga, & Associates, *Four stages of life: A comparative study of women and men facing transitions.* San Francisco: Jossey-Bass, 1975.

Lowenthal, M. F., Thurnher, M., Chiriboga, D., & Associates. *Four stages of life: A comparative study of women and men facing transitions.* San Francisco: Jossey-Bass, 1975.

Lowenthal, M. F., & Weiss, L. Intimacy and crises in adulthood. *Counseling Psychologist,* 1976, *6*(1), 10–15.

Maslow, A. *Motivation and personality.* New York: Harper, 1954.

Masters, W. H., & Johnson, V. E. *Human sexual response.* Boston: Little, Brown, 1966.

Meichenbaum, D. H. Cognitive factors in behavior modification: Modifying what clients say to themselves. In C. Franks & G. T. Wilson (Eds.), *Annual review of behavior therapy.* New York: Brunner/Mazel, 1973.

Miller, A. *System for identifying motivated abilities.* West Simsbury, Conn.: People Management, Inc., 1971.

Mischel, W. Sex-typing and personality. In P. H. Mussen (Ed.), *Carmichael's manual of childhood psychology* (Vol. 2). New York: John Wiley & Sons, 1970.

Neugarten, B. L. The awareness of middle age. In B. L. Neugarten (Ed.), *Middle age and aging.* Chicago: University of Chicago Press, 1968.

Neugarten, B. L. Adult personality: Toward a psychology of the life cycle. In B. L. Neugarten (Ed.), *Middle age and aging.* Chicago: University of Chicago Press, 1968.

Neugarten, B. L. Adaptation and the life cycle. *Counseling Psychologist,* 1976, *6*(1), 16–20.

Neugarten, B. L. Adaptation and the life cycle. In N. K. Schlossberg & A. D. Entine (Eds.), *Counseling adults.* Monterey, Calif.: Brooks/Cole, 1977.

Neugarten, B. L., & Garron, D. Attitudes of middle-aged persons toward growing older. *Geriatrics,* 1951, *14,* 21–24.

Neugarten, B. L., & Gutmann, D. L. Age-sex roles and

personality in middle age: A thematic apperception study. In B. L. Neugarten & Associates, *Personality in middle and late life*. New York: Atherton, 1964.

Neugarten, B. L., & Kraines, R. J. Menopausal symptoms in women of various ages. *Psychosomatic Medicine*, 1965, *27*, 266–273.

Neugarten, B. L., Moore, J. W., & Lowe, J. C. Age norms, age constraints, and adult socialization. *American Journal of Sociology*, 1965, *70*, 710–717.

Neugarten, B. L., & Weinstein, K. K. The changing American grandparent. *Journal of Marriage and the Family*, 1964, *26*, 199–204.

Nowak, C. *Concern with youthfulness and attractiveness in adult women*. Unpublished master's thesis, Wayne State University, 1974.

Nydegger, C. N. *Late and early fathers*. Paper presented at the Annual Meeting of the Gerontological Society, Miami Beach, Fla., November 1973.

Ochiltree, J. K., Brekke, D., & Yager, G. E. *A cognitive self-instructional modeling approach vs. the Carkhuff model for training empathy*. Paper presented at the meeting of the American Educational Research Association, Washington, D.C., 1975.

Parkes, C. M. Effects of bereavement on physical and mental health: A study of the medical records of widows. *British Medical Journal*, 1964, *2*, 274–279.

Parnes, H. S., Nestel, G., & Andrisani, P. *The pre-retirement years: A longitudinal study of the labor market experience of men* (Vol. 3). Columbus, Ohio: Center for Human Resource Research, 1972.

Pascal, A. H. *An evaluation of policy related research on programs for mid-life career redirections: Vol. 1. Executive summary* (Prepared for the National Science Foundation under Contract R-1582-1-NSF). Santa Monica, Calif.: Rand Corporation, 1975.

Pineo, P. C. Disenchantment in the later years of marriage. *Marriage and Family Living*, 1961, *23*, 3–11.

Powers, E., & Goudy, W. Examination of the meaning of work to older workers. *Aging and Human Development*, 1971, *2*, 38–45.

Project on the Status and Education of Women. *Women's centers: Where are they?* (Rev. ed.). Washington, D.C.: PSEW, Association of American Colleges, September 1975.

Quinn, R., Staines, G., & McCullough, M. *Job satisfaction: Is there a trend?* (U.S. Department of Labor, Manpower Research Monograph No. 30). Washington, D.C.: U.S. Government Printing Office, 1974.

Riegel, K. F. Developmental psychology and society: Some historical and ethical considerations. In J. R. Nesselroade & H. W. Reese (Eds.), *Life-span developmental psychology: Methodological issues*. New York: Academic Press, 1973.

Riley, M. W., Johnson, M., & Foner, A. (Eds.), *Aging and society* (3 vols.). New York: Russell Sage Foundation, 1968–1972.

Roe, A., & Baruch, R. *Factors influencing career decisions: A pilot study* (Harvard Studies in Career Development, No. 32). Cambridge, Mass.: Center for Research in Careers, Graduate School of Education, Harvard University, 1964.

Rosow, I. *Social integration of the aged*. New York: Free Press, 1967.

Rotter, J. Generalized expectancies for internal versus external control of reinforcement. *Psychological Monographs*, 1966, *80*(1, Whole No. 609).

Schaie, K. W. A reinterpretation of age-related changes in cognitive structure and functioning. In L. R. Goulet & P. B. Baltes (Eds.), *Life-span developmental psychology*. New York: Academic Press, 1970.

Schlossberg, N. K. Adult men: Education or re-education? *Vocational Guidance Quarterly*, 1972, *20*, 266–270.

Schlossberg, N. K., & Pietrofesa, J. Perspectives on counseling bias: Implications for counselor education. *Counseling Psychologist*, 1973, *4*(1), 44–54.

Scholz, N., Prince, J. S., & Miller, G. P. *How to decide: A guide for women*. New York: College Entrance Examination Board, 1975.

Shepard, H. Life planning program. In J. W. Pfeiffer & J. E. Jones (Eds.), *A handbook of structured experiences for human relations training* (Vol. 2, rev. ed.). San Diego, Calif.: University Associates, 1974.

Sheppard, D. I. The measurement of vocational maturity in adults. *Journal of Vocational Behavior*, October 1971, pp. 399–406.

Sheppard, H. L. *New perspectives on older workers*. Washington, D.C.: W.E. Upjohn Institute for Employment Research, 1971.

Sheppard, H. L., & Belitsky, A. H. *The job hunt*. Baltimore: Johns Hopkins Press, 1966.

Simon, S. B., Howe, L. W., & Kirschenbaum, H. *Values clarification: A handbook of practical strategies for teachers and students*. New York: Hart, 1972.

Sontag, S. The double standard of aging. *Saturday Review*, 23 September 1972, pp. 29–38.

Strong, E. K., Jr., & Campbell, D. P. *Strong-Campbell vocational interest blank.* Stanford, Calif.: Stanford University Press, 1974.

Sussman, M. B., & Burchinal, L. Kin family network: Unheralded structure in current conceptualizations of family functioning. *Marriage and Family Living,* 1962, *24*(3), 231–240.

Thurnher, M. Family confluence, conflict, and affect. In M. F. Lowenthal, M. Thurnher, D. Chiriboga, & Associates, *Four stages of life: A comparative study of women and men facing transitions.* San Francisco: Jossey-Bass, 1975.

Tiedeman, D. V., & O'Hara, R. P. *Career development: Choice and adjustment.* New York: College Entrance Examination Board, 1963.

Timiras, P. S. *Developmental physiology and aging.* New York: Macmillan, 1972.

Toffler, A. *Future shock.* New York: Random House, 1970.

Townsend, P. The emergence of the four-generation family in industrial society. In B. L. Neugarten (Ed.), *Middle age and aging.* Chicago: University of Chicago Press, 1968.

Treybig, D. *Language, children, and attitudes toward the aged: A longitudinal study.* Paper presented at the meeting of the Gerontological Society, Portland, Oregon, 1974.

Troll, L. E. *Early and middle adulthood: The best is yet to be—maybe.* Monterey, Calif.: Brooks/Cole, 1975.

Troll, L. E., & Nowak, C. "How old are you?" The question of age bias in the counseling of adults. *Counseling Psychologist,* 1976, *6*(1), 41–43.

Troll, L. E., & Schlossberg, N. K. How "age-biased" are college counselors? *Industrial Gerontology,* Summer 1971, pp. 14–20.

U.S. Department of Labor, Employment Standards Administration, Women's Bureau. *Continuing education for women: Current developments.* Washington, D.C.: Government Printing Office, 1974.

Veroff, J., & Feld, S. *Marriage and work in America: A study of motives and roles.* New York: Van Nostrand Reinhold, 1970.

Weiss, L., & Lowenthal, M. F. Life-course perspectives on friendship. In M. F. Lowenthal, M. Thurnher, D. Chiriboga, & Associates, *Four stages of life: A comparative study of women and men facing transitions.* San Francisco: Jossey-Bass, 1975.

Weiss, R. S. *Marital separation.* New York: Basic Books, 1975.

Weiss, R. S. Transition states and other stressful situations: Their nature and programs for their management. In G. Caplan & M. Killilea (Eds.), *Support systems and mutual help: Multidisciplinary explorations.* New York: Grune & Stratton, 1976.

White, R. *Lives in progress* (2nd ed.). New York: Holt, Rinehart & Winston, 1966.

Wilensky, H. L. Orderly careers and social participation: The impact of work history on social integration in the middle mass. *American Sociological Review,* 1961, *26* (4), 521–539.

Index